HELPING STUDENTS WRITE ...

The Best Research Reports Ever

Easy Mini-Lessons,
Strategies, and
Creative Formats
to Make Research
Manageable and Fun

By Lois Laase and Joan Clemmons

SCHOLASTIC
PROFESSIONAL BOOKS

New York • Toronto • London • Auckland • Sydney

ACKNOWLEDGMENTS

I want to thank my students at Rolling Valley School for allowing me to include their pictures, comments, and work samples.

I am grateful to Lois and Paul for their kind hospitality while Lois and I were writing the manuscript in their home.

To my husband, Rod, I want to express my deepest appreciation for his encouragement, patience, enthusiastic support, and assistance.

—Joan

• • • • • • • • • • •

I want to thank the students and staff, especially the fourth-grade team— Pat, Lin, and Pam—at Wingate Elementary for allowing me to include their comments, work samples, and pictures, and to extend a special thanks to Sandy Cruz for sharing her lessons and her insights on student learning.

My deepest gratitude goes to Tom Parrish for facilitating my schedule adjustments.

I also want to express my heartfelt appreciation to Pam Newton, my teaching partner, who shared many wonderful teaching strategies and who was always there with her friendship and support.

And to my husband, Paul, I want to express my deepest appreciation for his enduring and enthusiastic support.

—Lois

Primary sources and Web site boxes were adapted from a forthcoming
Scholastic Professional Book on using primary sources by Karen Baicker.

Cover design by Kathy Massaro
Interior design by Sydney Wright

ISBN 0-590-96386-4

Contents

CHAPTER SIX: DEVELOPING AND MAINTAINING ASSESSMENTS THAT ARE VALID AND LINKED TO CLASS INSTRUCTION

MAKING RESEARCH EXCITING AND MEANINGFUL

"**C**harles has his topic, but he doesn't know where or how to begin his research, and I don't know where to begin to help him." A mutual friend was telling us how frustrated she, as a parent, was with the research report her son was told to write. When we asked Charles about the report, he replied that he liked his topic but he didn't know what he was supposed to do.

We recalled feeling the same way as children when we were assigned to write a report on a country. For example, we remember going to the library and finding the shelf with all the encyclopedias. Then, with note cards in hand, we copied the information exactly as it was printed in the encyclopedia. This was our research. After putting the cards in some form of order, we copied them as our report.

Because research and report writing are difficult and complex tasks, we teachers need to guide students carefully through each step of the process. This book, in spite of thousands of miles separating us (Lois teaching fourth grade at Wingate Elementary school in Grand Junction, Colorado, and Joan teaching fifth grade at Rolling Valley Elementary School in Fairfax County, Virginia, where we first taught together), is the result of our combined classroom experience. Over time we've developed lessons that we've found to be effective for teaching the skills and strategies necessary for research and expository writing. The lessons have evolved as we've gone through the research process with our students many times, discovering what works and what doesn't work. Using the telephone, the information highway, and intense work sessions, we have collaborated to refine the successful lessons. As a result, our students have become excited and successful readers and writers of nonfiction.

Fifth-grader Marissa summed it up this way: "This year I learned how to research, how to write notes, and how to write great reports." What confidence she has in her ability as a

7

researcher and writer! Marissa is developing the lifelong skills she'll use as she writes nonfiction throughout her school years and her adult life.

We're excited about the research happening in our classrooms. In this book, in addition to sharing the lessons that have made our students successful researchers and writers, we'll provide lots of exciting strategies and projects you can use. Research, whether it is for writing a report, conducting an interview, creating a book, or completing another form of the many possible presentations, is a process—a journey—in which the students, with guidance, develop into independent learners as they learn how to learn.

• • • • • • • • •

Connecting Students' Natural Curiosity to Research

As the guests were leaving our ancient Egyptian museum, our fifth graders, dressed as ancient Egyptians, commented enthusiastically, "That was fun! When can we start our next research project? May we create another museum?" That's the attitude we always hope our students will have as they approach research, as opposed to the dread and fear we remember when we were young students and were told to write a research report. Students' natural curiosity and their desire to learn about the world around them are wonderful motivators for teaching research and expository writing.

To get students interested and actively engaged in research, it's important to make the process and the end goal as exciting as possible.

We've identified four ways to get our students excited about doing research: We allow them to work collaboratively; we have them become experts on their topics; we immerse them in a unit of study before they start their research; and we give them the opportunity to choose topics about which they are naturally curious.

> *Students' natural curiosity and their desire to learn about the world around them are wonderful motivators for teaching research and expository writing.*

Collaboration

When we tell students they can work together to research and develop a project on one aspect of an overall topic, such as the Egyptian museum, they are excited. For example, when we introduced the unit on ancient Egypt and asked the students if they would like to collaborate to develop a museum as a culminating activity for the unit, their eyes widened and, with pleasant expressions on their faces, shouted, "Yes!" They were ready to start right then. Working collaboratively helps overcome any fear of tackling the topic. (See Making Research

Come Alive With Museums and Festivals, Chapter Five, pages 109-111, for details on how the students worked collaboratively to research and develop a museum as a culminating activity for the unit of study.)

Expertise

When students realize their research will make them experts on a topic that they can then teach to others, they're motivated to learn all they can about their chosen topics.

Katie and Eun-Ji work collaboratively on their Egyptian Museum project.

Being recognized as authorities gives them a feeling of confidence and empowerment. When our students learned that they could use their research on Egypt to explain or teach the information they learned to other students and to their parents in the museum setting, they were thrilled.

Immersion

Immersing students in a unit of study for a while before they start the journey of researching a topic is vital in arousing their curiosity. They marvel at some of the information and ask questions as we read to them or as they examine print and nonprint materials in a unit interest center. They want answers to their questions. A guest speaker or a field trip may kindle the same kind of surprise and curiosity.

The KWL strategy is a favorite of ours to use early in a unit of study to inspire our students to think about what they want to learn. They brainstorm what they already know about the topic and what they want to learn about it. When the students think critically about what they want to find out as well as listen to the ideas of their classmates, they are eager to search for answers to their questions.

9

Choice

Research topics should not always be related to a unit of study. Children enjoy conducting inquiry searches on topics or questions that come up naturally and about which they are curious. Having students ponder about things they have a burning desire to know will elicit lots of ideas and questions for research.

For example, Jonathan said, "I've been looking at the Hale Bopp comet every night this week. What is it? What is a comet?"

Rachel and Jennifer work together as they research theater in Ancient Greece

Jonathan could hardly wait to begin the research process. He became our expert on comets and shared his findings in a question-and-answer book he wrote for his classmates. Laura remembered a family trip to Niagara Falls when she was very young. She said that she had always wondered about the falls and had many questions she wanted to answer. Upon completion of her research, she created a travel brochure for her classmates and for the school library. Jennifer was fascinated with wolves and could hardly wait to share with us the information she researched.

Research topics should not be determined by the teachers; students need to be a part of framing or creating these topics. When the students are allowed to choose their topics or questions to research— whether it is in a unit of study, or in a genre of writing being studied, or a subject they are wondering about— they become more actively involved in their learning and more directly engaged in inquiry.

Whether it's part of a unit of study, a genre of writing the class is exploring, or something that arises naturally, students need to be a part of deciding on research topics. When they are allowed to choose their topics or questions to research, they become more actively involved in their learning and more directly engaged in inquiry. They find that reading and writing non-fiction is an exciting and enjoyable way to learn.

As teachers, our role is to assist the students in their inquiry by stimulating their thinking and inspiring them to take charge of their learning, thus raising their motivation and feeling of ownership. We make sure to design focused mini-lessons that teach the skills and strategies the students need in order to be successful

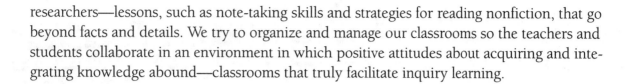

researchers—lessons, such as note-taking skills and strategies for reading nonfiction, that go beyond facts and details. We try to organize and manage our classrooms so the teachers and students collaborate in an environment in which positive attitudes about acquiring and integrating knowledge abound—classrooms that truly facilitate inquiry learning.

Overcoming the Reading Hurdle

Doing research is exciting for children, but not if they have difficulty reading the informational texts required. Many students find that nonfiction is much more difficult to read than fiction. Why? First, students don't have the background knowledge to read expository texts. They've heard stories from birth, so they're used to listening for a story line with characters. But expository writing has a different text structure and may contain technical and difficult vocabulary words that are critical for comprehension. So even though many students are attracted to nonfiction books, they need instruction in reading them for meaning. Not only will they need the ability to read expository texts for doing research, they'll need it for the majority of standardized test questions, as well as a large part of their reading in adult life—newspapers, magazines, directions, and so on.

> *Doing research is exciting for children, but not if they have difficulty reading their references. If we want students to use nonfiction when they research, we have to teach them how to read nonfiction.*

We've refined a number of techniques to use in teaching students to read nonfiction. These include read-alouds, think-alouds, buddy reading, point-of-view watch, and signal word recognition.

Read-Alouds

Since we read aloud to our students to strengthen the concepts we're teaching in various content areas, our read-alouds have also become our favorite tool for teaching the art of reading nonfiction. We know that students of all ages can benefit from read-alouds; they are not just for elementary students. Read-alouds familiarize students with the genre of nonfiction. They can be used to introduce new vocabulary and to support the necessary focused mini-lessons. As we read aloud in these lessons, we model using metacognition—that is, we think aloud or verbalize what we do when we read.

Think-Alouds

The strategies we verbalize as we read-aloud and think-aloud are similar to the ones students use when they're reading fiction. We've adapted and broadened them for reading nonfiction.

The Best Research Reports Ever *Scholastic Professional Books, 1998*

We start by modeling the following prereading strategies:

• *Discussing what we already know about the topic.* For instance, if we use the book *Why Don't You Get a Horse, Sam Adams?* by Jean Fritz (Scholastic, 1974) for our read-aloud, we ask our students to verbalize what they already know about Sam Adams. By assessing their prior knowledge, students can connect the new information they read to something they already know.

Lois Laase reads a nonfiction book aloud to a class of fourth graders.

• *Previewing the material to be read.* We show students how to look through the table of contents, read the headings, charts, graphs, and captions, study the pictures, and so on, to get an overview of the text.

• *Making predictions about the kind of information expected.* Predicting heightens interest in reading the text, encourages critical thinking, and helps students become personally involved with the text.

• *Asking questions before reading.* This technique gives students a focus for reading. If there are headings, we show students how to use them to formulate the questions. As we read, we look for answers to the questions.

Rereading for meaning is a strategy that students often don't use when reading nonfiction, but they discover it to be the most beneficial.

Important strategies to use while reading include retelling and rereading. We have students stop at strategic places and retell in their own words what has just been read. If students have trouble putting it in their own words, we have them reread the section and then retell. If they still experience difficulty retelling, we show them how to read an even shorter passage before retelling. Retelling shows the students—and the teacher—whether they've understood what they've read. Students frequently neglect to use the rereading-for-meaning strategy when they read nonfiction, but it's the one they usually discover to be the most beneficial.

Jonathan put it this way on his self-evaluation: "I have improved in reading this year. I am now reading 45 minutes a night, and I am enjoying reading. I am reading harder books that are longer, so I have to use my reading strategies to understand what I am reading. The two strategies I use most are asking questions and retelling what I read. If I can't retell what I've read, I go back and reread."

Other reading strategies we introduce to students include how to use the context to determine the meaning of unfamiliar words, how to use the glossary and dictionary, and how to relate new information to what they already know. We model the after-reading strategies of summarizing the text in their own words and thinking about and trying to answer the questions they asked at the prereading stage. We've developed a think-aloud worksheet, "Strategies for Reading Nonfiction," (see page 14) that lists all the reading strategies. Our students use it as they practice and perfect their expository reading skills.

Buddy Reading

After we've modeled two or three strategies, we have our students read with a buddy and practice verbalizing what they're thinking, just as we did. As students work together, we move from group to group giving assistance as needed or acting as a buddy for a student. We focus on the students with the greatest needs by remodeling the strategies and questioning and prompting them to practice the strategies at appropriate times. Students use the think-aloud worksheet to record their progress.

Ryan and Andrew practice nonfiction reading strategies as they read a weekly news magazine together.

We model and walk students through these strategies many times throughout the year. We want our students to use these strategies independently to understand the materials they're reading as they do research and to answer their research questions. We're not only teaching students to read nonfiction but to read to answer their research questions. Stacie, a college student helping out in our classrooms, commented, "I was never aware of some of these reading strategies. If I'd been taught them when I was in middle school, I'd have been a much better reader."

The Best Research Reports Ever *Scholastic Professional Books, 1998*

Strategies for Reading Nonfiction

Reader's Name .... Listener's Name ....

Title of Text .... Date ....

Listener's Checklist

Place a check next to the strategy each time it is verbalized.

Before Reading

.... Discusses what he/she already knows about the topic

.... Previews the text

.... Asks questions

.... Makes predictions

While Reading

.... Asks questions

       .... Uses headings to form questions

       .... Uses topic sentences to form questions

.... Looks for answers to questions

.... Checks for meaning by rereading the parts that he/she doesn't understand

.... Uses context clues to determine a new word or meaning of a word

.... Retells parts of the text

.... Rereads text if he/she can't retell

.... Notes the meanings of bold-faced words

.... Relates what is being read to prior knowledge

After Reading

.... Summarizes or retells the important things in the text

.... Thinks about the questions he/she had and tries to answer them

The Listener's comments: ....

....

The Best Research Reports Ever *Scholastic Professional Books, 1998*

Point-of-View Watch

In addition to being able to read for meaning, students need to understand that authors may write about a subject from varying points of view. They need to know that each author brings his own personal background of knowledge and experiences to his writing. As students use multiple sources in their research, we help them recognize how the points of view of authors might differ. For example, we may discuss the plight of endangered species from several points of view. Or we may compare points of view of British and American artists by examining different paintings of the Boston Massacre. We also select a current news story and discuss several points of view from which the story might have been written.

Signal Word Recognition

Another difficulty students have in reading informational texts is determining what is important. We show them how to recognize the words authors use to cue the reader that something important is going to happen or that signal a relationship between ideas. As students become aware of these words, they become more proficient readers of expository texts and are better able to determine important ideas they need to include in their research.

SIGNAL WORDS

Cause/Effect	Sequential Order	Comparing/Contrasting
therefore	first	as well as
because	secondly	similarly
because of	for example	while
as a result of	for instance	either...or
since	afterward	in comparison
consequently	next	in contrast
accordingly	to begin with	like
hence	in fact	rather than
thus	also	on the other hand
as a consequence	then	not only...but also
this is the reason why	since	although
so that	after that	but
otherwise	in the end	however
nevertheless	while	unless
	meanwhile	besides
	before	nevertheless
	finally	though
	another	nonetheless
	until	
	originally	
	in the beginning	
	initially	

The Best Research Reports Ever *Scholastic Professional Books, 1998*

Discovering the Forms of Writing

In our youth we thought that the encyclopedia was the only reference resource available to us, but we certainly don't want our students to think that way. We want to expose them to the many types of nonfiction writing used in expository text and to show them that their own presentations of research can take many forms. To help our students become acquainted with the diversity of writing styles in informational texts, we display a variety of texts on a number of topics. As students peruse the books, we ask them where they think the author got the information, the kinds of questions the book might answer, and how the author presented the information.

Greg checks out the forms of writing in various nonfiction materials.

Did you ever stop to think about the many ways non-fiction writing is presented? Students don't have to be limited to writing the traditional report.

The students are amazed there are so many different types of nonfiction books. Among the collection they discover biographies and photo biographies as well as picture books with very little writing. They love Jerry Pallotta's great ABC books and discover an unusual style—a diary written by a woman traveling in a covered wagon. We not only want them to see the different forms of expository writing found in the books they'll be using for research but to discover the different ways they'll be able to approach their own expository writing. The following list contains the variety of forms of nonfiction our students discovered.

16

TYPES OF NONFICTION

ABC books	Travel brochures	Diaries
Videos	Photos and captions	Speeches
Biographies	Fact and fiction	Questions and answers
Interviews	Headings and discussions	Time lines
Historical fiction	Narratives	Directions—How-to books
Essays	Picture books	Summaries
Magazine articles	Plays	Cartoons
Filmstrips	Big books	Travel logs
Poetry	Editorials	Encyclopedias
Recipes		

Did you ever stop to think about the many ways nonfiction writing is presented? Students don't have to be limited to writing the traditional report. Just as we use our fiction trade books as models to help students write their own fiction, we use nonfiction trade books and materials as models for students when they're writing nonfiction.

Once we've gotten our students excited about finding and researching a topic and have made sure they know how to read nonfiction, it's time to teach the skills they'll need to do the actual research. In the next chapter, we'll detail how we help our students understand the formats of books and other reference materials, so they'll know how to use them.

The Best Research Reports Ever *Scholastic Professional Books, 1998*

MINI-LESSONS TO TEACH BASIC RESOURCE INFORMATION AND SKILLS

Knowing how to locate reference material is paramount to success in any type of research project. Our young researchers experience less frustration when they know where and how to locate references and how to find the material they need within that reference. We've developed some quick-and-easy, motivating mini-lessons to help our students with the task. You can use these lessons with the whole class or with small groups who have similar needs. We never teach these lessons in isolation. We weave them through the research activities and teach them as often as necessary.

Mini-Lesson: Discovering the Tools of the Book

OBJECTIVE:

To have students discover the different parts of resource books and know how to use these parts effectively.

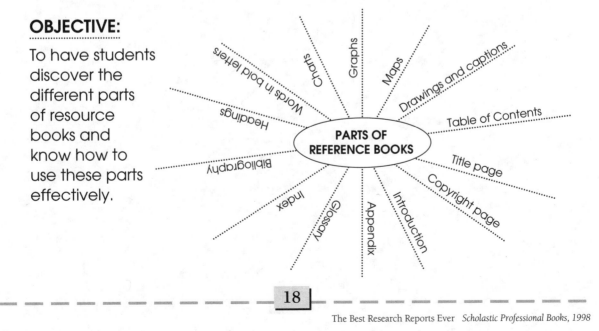

The Best Research Reports Ever *Scholastic Professional Books, 1998*

Getting Started—Assemble Resources

To prepare for this mini-lesson, we assemble a large variety of reference books from the library and from our own personal book collections. We want students to skim through these books to locate for themselves the different parts that can be used in research. Reading level is not an issue, although we try to find books at all levels. We also search for topics that will stimulate the interests of our students. Going well beyond the encyclopedia, we include photo books, how-to books, question-and-answer books, and other trade books, as well as the basic textbooks.

ACTIVITY: Reference Book Detectives

We pass out the reference books to the students and try, if possible, to give them books that match their interests and reading levels. This isn't necessary, but it's easier to motivate students' interest when the books intrigue them.

Students love games and love to be actively involved, so we make them all detectives for the day. Their task is to search for the different parts of the book. We give them a few minutes to look through the books, working with a neighbor if they wish. At first it is quiet, but as students locate the index, table of contents, and headings, the room fills with learning noise. As students make their discoveries, we summarize them on a huge web on the chalkboard, writing "Parts of Reference Books" in the center and the names of the parts on the legs.

The first time we did this, we made a fancy chart but only left ourselves room to draw a few spokes. We didn't realize how involved the students would get and how many different parts of a book they would discover. Now we use the chalkboard so that we can write large and add spokes as needed. Later on, students can copy this chart on fadeless paper or something similar and display it in the room.

As students name the parts of the book, or after most of the major parts have been mentioned, we discuss each one and decide how, or whether, it can be used to help us locate information. On page 20 you'll find a list and definitions of the different parts of a reference book. We post this for students to refer to, and we give each student a copy.

Aaron and Garrett become reference book detectives as they discover parts of the book that will help them do research.

PARTS OF REFERENCE BOOKS

Title page is usually the first printed page in a book. It gives the title of the book, the author's name, the publisher, and the place of publication.

Copyright page is right after the title page. It gives the year the book was published. If the book is old, it may not be a good source to use.

Introduction—also the preface, foreword, or acknowledgment—comes before the table of contents. It tells what the book is about.

Table of contents shows you the divisions of the book. It might be divided into chapters or units.

Body is the main text of the book.

Appendix comes after the body. It contains special information such as maps, charts, tables, letters, diagrams, and so on.

Glossary is at the end of the book. It is the dictionary part that defines specific words that are found in the book.

Bibliography is a list of books or articles that the author used as references when writing the book. It can help you find other books or references that might be useful for your research.

Index is an alphabetical listing of words and terms that are found in the book. It is a very helpful part of the book when you are looking for specific information.

Headings can be found in each chapter. They are titles that tell you what information can be located in that section of the chapter.

Bold-faced words are words that have been printed in bold type so that the reader can tell at a glance what is important on the page.

Most parts of reference books are easy for students to use; however, we find that they need guided practice in using the index and table of contents.

Mini-Lesson: Using the Index

OBJECTIVE:

To have students understand that when a comma comes after each page number in a series, it means the information is found only on each of those pages, and a dash between two numbers tells us that the information can be found on all the pages between and including those numbers.

Liam expressed frustration after reading throughout our science period to find out about water pipits. He said that he could find very little information in the book although he had read from page 14 to page 42. Unfortunately for Liam, he didn't notice or realize that there was a comma between the numbers 14 and 42 and that all he needed to read were those two pages! The dashes and commas can be very confusing to students. This lesson is designed to help students like Liam use the index effectively.

Getting Started—Locate Sample Indexes

To keep this lesson moving, we choose reference books that we have several copies of and make transparencies of the indexes. It's important that the indexes you choose have multiple examples of commas and dashes.

ACTIVITY: Search and Find

We project one of the transparencies on the overhead projector (see example on page 22) and ask, "Where in this book can you find information about boa constrictors?" We give the textbook to the student who answers and ask him to check pages 36, 38, and 67 to see if there is information about boas. We continue by asking "Do you think there is information about boas on page 37?" We then give another copy of the book to another student to check to see if information can be found on page 37. With just these two questions, the students realize that when a comma comes after each number, it means that the information can be found only on each of those pages. We continue our search-and-find activity until we are certain that students understand how commas after page numbers and dashes between numbers work in indexes.

The Best Research Reports Ever *Scholastic Professional Books, 1998*

INDEX

The Best Research Reports Ever *Scholastic Professional Books, 1998*

Students sometimes have difficulty thinking of synonyms for words they are researching. We use the same index to help them. We ask, "Where do boas live?" Frequently students respond that there isn't any information in this book to answer that question. To encourage them to delve further, we ask them to think of other words that might answer the question. "Home" and "country" are frequent replies, but they're not found in the index. We then encourage students to skim through the index to see if there's a word we haven't thought of. When they come upon the word *range*,

Nikki uses an index as a reference tool.

some students realize that this might work, especially since it has the word *geographic* written after it. We stress with our students that they have to be creative in thinking of synonyms for key words that might help them locate information.

• • • • • • • • •

Mini-Lesson: Using the Table of Contents

OBJECTIVE:

To enable students to scan quickly through a table of contents to see if the book contains reference material they can use and to illustrate that some tables of contents are more useful than others.

Getting Started—Locate Samples of Tables of Contents

To familiarize our students with different types of tables of contents, we take examples from several reference books and make transparencies of them so that all the students can see and refer to them. Some tables of contents list only a title of each chapter, whereas others include subheadings and are quite detailed. Be sure to include both in your samples.

The Best Research Reports Ever *Scholastic Professional Books, 1998*

ACTIVITY: Where Would You Find the Information?

After placing a transparency of a table of contents on the overhead projector, we have the students read it and try to determine the type of book from which it came. This brief activity helps them become familiar with how words are written in the table of contents. We always use reference materials that relate to our present unit of study so that students can see the connection. We begin by asking specific questions: "In which chapter could you find information about the life cycle of the porcupine?" or "In which chapter could I find information about a porcupine's diet?" To keep all students actively involved, we then have them turn to their neighbors and ask each other questions. We continue this activity until we feel certain that students are comfortable with scanning a table of contents to locate information. We repeat the activity with students who are still having trouble.

• • • • • • • • • •

Mini-Lesson: Searching for References

OBJECTIVE:

To discover the many references available for research and to complete a list of these sources.

"I can't find anything about John Elway. I looked in the card catalog, in the encyclopedia, and in all the books in our room." Comments like Peter's prompted us to develop a way to help our students discover the various reference sources available for research. Since John Elway is a contemporary professional football player, playing in the 1980s and 1990s, Peter couldn't find information about him in the textbook. But where could he find information about a modern-day athlete?

Getting Started—Check Out the Libraries

We always take the time to do our own research before we get our students involved in this mini-lesson. Besides searching through our school library, we make a trip to the public library to check out the reference materials available there. We learn something new every year, especially in the area of computerized research where the wealth of reference materials on CD-ROMS and on the Internet continues to increase. The Internet is a wonderful reference tool; however, it needs to be used carefully. Many innocent sounding search words can lead students into Web sites where they should not be. And it can be time consuming, especially for the students who are not familiar with Web searches. When possible, we monitor students' use of the Internet, but we still find that students can spend two hours or more searching Web sites for information and come up empty handed.

WHAT ARE PRIMARY SOURCES?

Primary sources are accounts by eyewitnesses or participants who record an event or their reactions to it during or immediately following its occurrence. These records may include objects or artifacts gathered at the event and documents of the event. The accounts may be:

written	printed	painted or drawn
photographed	mapped	tape recorded
filmed	video-taped	computer generated

When students utilize original sources in their research, they find the pulse and breath of people long dead, and they begin to be curious about these people—to empathize with them and to care about their fate. This exciting personal connection stimulates more research, more intense learning, and better retention of what students have learned

Students need to be aware that a primary source is not always any more reliable than a secondary source. The accounts frequently reflect a source's point of view, bias, or self-interest or are marred by confused memory or poor eyesight or hearing. Never-the-less, primary sources contain exciting pieces of the whole picture that can be considered and compared with others when doing research. Since they're available in such a wide variety of media, they're effective learning tools for all students, whatever their learning style.

Since this mini-lesson involves active student participation in the library, we schedule a day there when the librarian will be available to assist. We also enlist volunteers to give students the help and encouragement many of them need.

Checking Background Knowledge

"If I were doing a report on black bears, where would I look for information?" In response to this question, students begin throwing out their ideas. Jennifer says, "You could look in the encyclopedia." Aaron offers, "I know there are books on bears in the library; you could check one out." Students' responses are providing us with a check on their background knowledge. Having quickly stimulated student interest, we begin a chart of research resources:

> **Research Resources**
> Encyclopedias
> Books

We will add to the chart as we discover new sources. (See page 27 for an extended list.)

The Best Research Reports Ever *Scholastic Professional Books, 1998*

Scavenger Hunt—Group Search for Reference Material

The next stage of this lesson is a scavenger hunt for reference materials in the library. Before leaving for the library, we divide the students into groups of two or three and assign each group a topic. The purpose of this trip is not to do actual research; rather, it is for the scavenger hunters to practice finding reference materials that relate to their topics. We choose topics carefully, making sure each group has a different topic that will provide plenty of reference sources to discover.

Effective Reference Search Topics

A famous athlete (John Elway)	A state (Virginia)	A famous inventor (Alexander Graham Bell)
An animal (llama)	A former president (John F. Kennedy)	A disease (chicken pox)
A country (Japan)	A planet (Jupiter)	A sport (ice hockey)
An Indian tribe (Sioux)		

With notebooks in hand, we set off for the library. The librarian reviews the layout of the library, explains how the reference materials are shelved, shows students where the picture files are kept, and goes over the rules for using the Internet. Students then begin their search, carefully writing down where they locate information—not the information itself. We, the librarian, and the volunteers float from group to group suggesting new places to look for information and helping those who need it. After students appear to have located many

Ryan and Greg locate reference materials for their scavenger hunt topic.

The Best Research Reports Ever *Scholastic Professional Books, 1998*

references, we regroup, share, and add reference sources to the chart we began earlier in the classroom. We then give the students another 15 minutes to explore sources classmates discovered or to continue investigating new sources. Finally, we regroup again and once more add references to our chart.

Discovering Other Sources

For a homework assignment, we have the students ask their parents or friends where else they might go for information on their scavenger hunt topic. This strategy helps them realize that parents or family members are good sources and that they could interview doctors or other people in the community or visit a museum, zoo, or other sites to get more information. We want them to discover that they can use people and observation in addition to print as references.

Usually we only have to present this mini-lesson once, since students can always look at the chart when they need ideas for additional references. We never stop adding new reference sources to our chart, especially the nonlibrary sources we get from field trips and from writing to museums, embassies, and so on.

The students are amazed when we begin listing the possible sources they can use for research. Although this list is long, we know we missed some categories of sources.

Research Resources		
almanacs	encyclopedias	newspapers
atlases	field trips	papers
audiotapes	films	people
books	filmstrips	picture files
card catalog	graphs	radio programs
catalogs	historical records	readers' guides
CD-ROMs	Internet sites	slides
charts	interviews	television programs
comics	kits	textbooks
dictionaries	magazines	travel agencies
directories	maps	videotapes
embassies	museums	

The Best Research Reports Ever *Scholastic Professional Books, 1998*

CHECKLIST FOR LOCATING HISTORICAL RECORDS

Historical records are some of the best primary sources for students to explore when doing research. Here are some guidelines for where to look:

Just Looking

- municipal/county historian's office
- historical societies and museums
- state, local, and school libraries
- attics and basements
- local records repositories
- university library/special collections
- flea markets/bookshops featuring old books
- churches and temples

Looking for Specific Records

Personal papers *(diaries, letters, and so on)*
- archives
- historical societies
- family attics
- libraries (including state and university)

Business records *(executive, financial, employee records, and so on)*
- advertisements in old magazines
- old catalogs (1902 Sears Roebuck, for example)
- local historical society
- corporate archives
- state libraries
- local business people

Local government records *(court records, minutes of board meetings, deeds, school district records, military records, license permits, wills)*
- town clerk's office
- state archives
- local government archives
- local public schools
- surrogate courts (wills, inventories, and so on)

Census records
Federal (1790–1920)
- National Archives
- depository libraries

State
- country clerk's office
- libraries
- Genealogical Society of Utah, 50 East North Temple, Salt Lake City, Utah 84150

Death records, wills, inventories
- county clerk's office
- surrogate court

Organizational records *(labor unions, political parties, reform organizations, social clubs)*
- state, university, local libraries
- historical societies
- organizations themselves

Newspapers
- libraries
- museum collections

Photographs, postcards, posters
- historical societies
- museums
- archives
- state libraries
- depository libraries
- family albums
- garage sales, auctions

Based on list developed by Thomas Gray and Susan Owens,

The Best Research Reports Ever   *Scholastic Professional Books, 1998*

WORKSHEET FOR ANALYZING A WRITTEN DOCUMENT

Original documents are great primary sources for students' research. But if students don't know what to look for, the documents can be confusing. The following checklist will help them make the best use of documents they may discover as they explore their topic.

Type of Document (Check one):

__ Newspaper	__ Letter	__ Patent	__ Memorandum
__ Map	__ Telegram	__ Press release	__ Report
__ Advertisement	__ Congressional record	__ Census report	__ Other

Unique Physical Qualities of the Document (Check one or more):

__ Interesting letterhead	__ Handwritten	__ Notations
__ "RECEIVED" stamp	__ Other	

Date(s) of the document _____

Author or creator of the document _____

For what audience was the document written? _____

Document Information (There are many possible ways to answer.)

List three important features or points of the document. _____

_____

Why do you think this document was written? _____

_____

What evidence in the document helps you know why it was written? (Quote from the

document.) _____

_____

List two things the document tells you about life at the time it was written. _____

_____

Write a question to the author that is left unanswered by the document. _____

_____

_____

The Best Research Reports Ever   *Scholastic Professional Books, 1998*

Mini-Lesson: Culling Available Material

OBJECTIVE:

To help students learn to determine which sources may be useful for their research and which ones to discard without reading.

Getting Started— Gather a Variety of Reference Material

To model this lesson, we choose a research topic such as ice hockey and gather reference materials that relate to sports—the encyclopedia, sports books, books specifically about hockey, sports magazines, and so on. Then we make transparencies of the tables of contents and indexes.

Jonathan and Adam search the Internet for research information on their topic.

Looking for Clues

A little drama helps this lesson along. We pretend that we're frustrated because we have so many references and that we simply don't know where to begin. We moan and groan a bit and then ask students if they can help us. We hold up the different books and ask students to help us decide from just the clues in the titles whether they think each book will include information about ice hockey. Together, we decide that if a book's title has the word *hockey* in it, it should be worth investigating. We lead students to realize that the book about track and field probably doesn't have any information about hockey and we can discard it. We see that a book that's about all sports may be worth a look at the table of contents or the index to see if hockey or ice hockey are mentioned. Students flip

Determining which references contain pertinent information on a topic is an important skill students need to achieve before tackling the research process.

The Best Research Reports Ever *Scholastic Professional Books, 1998*

through the books that don't have either a table of contents or index, looking for clues such as pictures or headings. Next, we show students the sports magazines. They help us skim through the tables of contents for articles specifically about ice hockey.

This lesson involves a lot of discussion among students as they try to help us determine which material we should keep and which we should discard without reading. We want our students to become experts at culling material so they can weed through a long list of magazine articles they might find when they use the *Reader's Guide to Periodical Literature* or search the mass of information on the Internet. This is not an easy concept to teach, and students need guidance and experience with it before tackling the research process.

• • • • • • • • • •

Once students have gained the basic skills of locating the materials they'll use to learn about their topic, they're ready to begin their research, and we begin teaching mini-lessons that help them use the materials.

CHAPTER 3

MINI-LESSONS TO DEVELOP TOP-NOTCH RESEARCHERS

We and our students have had wonderful experiences with research and research projects. Besides the Egyptian museum, we've presented a Greek play, developed a TV interview show with interviews of historical figures, created a question-and-answer book on dinosaurs, and many more projects. Once they get involved with these kinds of projects, our students are excited and so are we. But it hasn't always been that way. After assigning countless research projects, we realized that we were expecting our students to have the skills of researchers without giving them any on-the-job training. We saw that if we wanted them to become competent researchers, we'd have to provide the training and guide them through the process.

We began to succeed when we developed a logical, well-organized yearlong plan for teaching research. Now we begin early in the year with lessons and practice on note-taking, using the research materials from our social studies or science units. We don't expect major written projects until our students are comfortable with taking and organizing notes. Still, since we want to connect the note-taking with a real purpose, we begin by having students use their notes to create short oral reports, radio interviews, and smaller written projects such as travel brochures. This allows students to begin to develop confidence in their ability to research. Toward the end of the school year they're excited about writing a research paper and ready to begin. Following are the mini-lessons and practice projects our students need to become top-notch researchers.

Mini-Lesson: Note-Taking Strategies for Text

OBJECTIVE:

To help students write effective notes from text.

"We shouldn't plagiarize." Students know these words mean something about not copying directly from a book, but many don't know how else to take notes. Good note-taking skills are vital to researching and writing reports, and we've found that the key to success in teaching these skills is to teach them when the students need them and not as an isolated lesson. That's why we relate them to the units students are studying.

Getting Started—Choose Sample Paragraphs

To get ready for this lesson, we select sample paragraphs from material relating to our current unit—for example, whales in a science unit on marine life. We choose paragraphs from textbooks and supplementary texts, enlarge the print, and make transparencies so we can show them on the overhead. We frequently copy paragraphs from CD-ROM material because it's easy to cut and paste a group of paragraphs together and then enlarge them on-screen before printing them out.

MODELING: Taking Notes From Text

Before we show the transparencies, we ask, "What do you know about note-taking?" As students respond, we chart their comments:

What I Know About Note-Taking
> Keep it short.
> Don't copy.
> Write what is important.

Now that we've peaked their interest, it's time to model how to write notes in your own words. As with reading strategies, we find that the best way to model note-taking skills is to think aloud as we read from a text and write notes. For example, for our study on whales, we project a transparency of a paragraph from Seymour Simon's book, *Whales*.

> *A fish breathes by taking in water and passing it through gills to extract oxygen, but a whale must surface to inhale air into its lungs. A whale's nostril, called a blowhole, is at the top of its head. A whale breathes through its blowhole. Some whales, such as the humpback, have two blowholes. Here they are open, as the humpback whale exhales old air and inhales fresh oxygen-rich air.*
> —Seymour Simon, *Whales*, HarperCollins Publishers, 1989.

The Best Research Reports Ever *Scholastic Professional Books, 1998*

After reading the paragraph aloud to the students, we go back to the beginning and say what we're thinking as we read: "This paragraph is about how a whale breathes. This first sentence tells me that a whale doesn't breathe like a fish; it has lungs." We draw lines under the words *surface*, *inhale*, and *lungs*. We continue reading through the paragraph, underlining the key words and thinking aloud about the important point in each sentence. We explain to students that the words we're underlining are important details about how a whale breathes.

Next, on a sheet of chart paper we write "How Whales Breathe," the paragraph's main topic, and jot down the supporting details. We emphasize that we are using our own words and encourage students to compare our notes to the written text to see how they are not the same.

> **How Do Whales Breathe?**
> • fish breathe through gills
> • whales breathe through lungs
> • whales surface to inhale
> • nostrils are blowholes
> • humpbacks have two blowholes

Practice: Taking Notes From Text

Next, we put another paragraph from *Whales* on the overhead projector and read it aloud.

> *The air that whistles in and out of a whale's blowhole moves at speeds of two or three hundred miles an hour. It enters and leaves the lungs, within the whale's chest. With each breath, a whale inhales thousands of times more air than you do. The whale closes its blowhole and holds its breath when it dives. Some kinds of whales can dive to depths as great as a mile and hold their breath for more than an hour during a deep dive. When they surface, they blow out a huge breath and then take several smaller breaths before diving again.*

This time, we want students to be active participants. We invite them to help discover the passage's topic and the supporting ideas. We underline the key words they choose as we reread the paragraph. And as they help us choose the main idea and the supporting details, we list these on another sheet of chart paper.

> **How Whales Breathe**
> • air enters lungs at 2 or 3 hundred miles per hour
> • closes blowhole when diving
> • dives a mile down
> • holds breath for an hour

The Best Research Reports Ever *Scholastic Professional Books, 1998*

Then we turn off the overhead projector and have students work with a buddy to summarize the paragraph in their own words.

Now we ask students to suggest guidelines they'd like to add to our how-to-take-notes chart. We provide prompts such as "How do you select the topic of the paragraph?" or "What do you think about as you read the sentences of the paragraph?" We hang the note-taking chart in the classroom and add ideas to it as students learn other note-taking strategies. Students use the chart as a reference all year long as they do research.

What I Know About Note-Taking

- It is short.
- Do not copy the author's sentences.
- Write down what is important.
- Use your own words, not the author's words.
- Reread the paragraph and write the topic.
- Write the important ideas that tell about the topic.
- Make sure the notes are organized by topic.
- It's what the book is about.

Next, we have students work together in small groups to practice the note-taking skill. We give each group a copy of another paragraph about marine life. Together, they determine the main idea of the paragraph and the important details. It's always important to remind students to underline the key words. This helps them rewrite the important points in their own words. We always move from group to group, giving encouragement and assistance: "Great job, I want you to share those notes with the rest of the class."

A seventh grader uses her note-taking skills to do her research on Egypt.

The Best Research Reports Ever *Scholastic Professional Books, 1998*

"You really are picking out the main ideas."

When most groups are finished, we call the whole class together and ask a few groups to share their notes. We encourage other groups to respond and interact. Did the group list the important ideas? Did they identify the topic of the paragraph? Did they use their own words when they wrote the key ideas?

When students are active learners and active investigators, note-taking is fun and easy. They don't need to plagiarize.

A group of students worked together to write these notes from a book on Egypt.

Houses in Ancient Egypt

- Built out of bricks
- Mud came from the Nile River
- Mud was put in leather buckets then took to where houses being built
- People put straw and pebles in the mud to make the mud stronger
- mud put into wooden frames to make bricks
- The workers left the bricks in the sun
- Plaster was put on walls
- Inside was painted with or somethings from nature
- houses were not that hot
- windows bearly let light through
- rich families had big houses

• • • • • • • • • •

Mini-Lesson: Note-Taking Strategies for Oral Presentations

OBJECTIVE:

To help students take effective notes from oral presentations.

Besides knowing how to take notes from text presentations, students need to learn to take notes as they listen to speakers, see videos or filmstrips, or when they are conducting interviews. This is a different kind of note-taking. Speakers tend to talk fast and cover many topics in a short time, and students have to learn how to pick out the main ideas as they listen and to quickly jot down words or phrases that will prompt their memories later.

Well-organized notes help students complete well-organized research papers or projects.

The Best Research Reports Ever *Scholastic Professional Books, 1998*

Getting Started—Arrange for Speakers or Videos

As our students start studying a unit on local history or electricity, for example, we book speakers and acquire videos on the topic. Before we show the video or before the speaker arrives, we prepare students with some background information.

MODELING: Listening for the Main Ideas

Before the speaker begins, we tell our students that we're going to learn about how to take notes on a speech but that this time they should just listen to the speaker and not write anything. For instance, after a local cattle

Vanessa takes notes as she listens to a speaker.

rancher speaks to our class, we gather and discuss all the ideas we remember. We begin by asking questions: "What were the main points of the rancher's speech?" "What was the purpose of his speech?" As students talk, we write key ideas on the chalkboard. One student says that he discussed how cattle are branded. Another student says that he discussed why cattle are branded. We encourage students to save their discussions of the details until we've recorded the main ideas. We agree to write "branding" as one of the major points of the speech, leaving the details of why and how until later. Students suggest that calving was another major topic. Once the main points have been recalled, we ask students for details. As they talk, we write key words or phrases such as "branding iron" and "tells ownership" under "branding." This process helps students realize that there's an order to the speaker's remarks.

Plains Life Zone

Plains Life Zone
lowest altitude -3300 ft
little snow - rain
gas C + W

Trees - Plants
willow
cottonwood
ceeder
yucka
peron-pine
cactus
buffalo grass
gramma grass
stick weed
milkweed
rabbit brush

Fourth grader Adrienne wrote these notes after viewing and listening to an oral presentation on the Colorado Plains life zone.

The Best Research Reports Ever *Scholastic Professional Books, 1998*

Plains Life Zone

The plains life zone has the lowest altitude in Colorado. There is very little rain and snow and it is very very dry. It is on both east and west sides, the plains lowest altitude is 3300 feet.

There are many kinds of trees on the plains. Some of them are; willows, cottenwoods, ceeder, yucha and piñon pine. There are many plants too; cactus, buffalo grass, grumma grass, stick weed, Milkweed, rabbit brush, and probably many others.

Plains have all kinds of animals on them like; buffalo, cyotes, prong horn-antilope, deer, rattle snakes and lizards, white tailed deer, jack rabbits and many others. There are lots of birds to like Geese and many kinds of ducks, halks, owls, meadowlarks, pheasants and our state bird the Lark Bunting.

The plains also have many kinds of crops a couple of them are; wheat and fruit and vegitables.

We also have recreation like. Hot air balooning and boating there are a lot more though.

Plains soil is clayish

Adrienne turned her notes into this report on the plains life zone.

PRACTICE
Writing Main Ideas

The next time students view a video or hear a speaker, we again have them listen without writing during the presentation. This time, however, we have students work in small groups of three or four to write their notes. We move from group to group, giving encouragement or stopping to help the learners who need more guidance.

This modeling and practicing continues until the students feel comfortable noting what they recall after they've heard an oral presentation. It doesn't take many guided lessons before our students can sit with a pad of paper and pencil and take notes while they listen to a speaker. They learn to listen for the key ideas and jot down only words and phrases, paraphrasing what they hear.

The note-taking mini-lessons flow naturally into the next lesson on organizing research notes.

• • • • • • • • • •

Mini-Lesson: Data Retrieval Chart/ Note-Taking Grid

OBJECTIVE:

To help students develop and use a system for taking notes and organizing research.

> "My data retrieval chart helped me write all of my great reports. It helps me organize my notes and write them without copying from a book."

This is a comment Marissa wrote in an end-of-the-year letter to her parents. The data retrieval chart she refers to is our favorite way for students to organize their information. The chart,

The Best Research Reports Ever *Scholastic Professional Books, 1998*

which we call a note-taking grid or research grid, involves students in using a large-scale grid to categorize facts from several sources. As students complete their grids, they can see at a glance the information they have and areas in which they need to do more research.

We've found that the individual note-taking grids are far more successful for taking and organizing notes than the traditional index card. No longer do our students carry around stacks of file cards bound with a rubber band; instead, their notes are organized on one sheet. When students have a specific but simple format to use for their notes, doing research is fun—not an onerous task. And well-organized notes keep students focused on their topic and help them complete well-organized research papers or projects. (For more information on group data retrieval charts, see *Language Arts Mini-Lessons* by Joan Clemmons and Lois Laase; Scholastic, 1995).

A data retrieval chart is a large-scale grid that enables students to categorize facts from several sources.

Getting Started—Choice of a Topic and a Grid for Each Student

Before students begin their research and before we start modeling, we choose a topic for research and gather reference materials for it. It's important to choose a topic that fits with what your students are researching. For example, when our class was researching famous American women, we chose Helen Keller as the example for our chart. A teacher of a middle-school class has her students researching specific countries, so she chooses a country when she models the procedure. Once we have some reference materials, we copy paragraphs from several different references onto transparencies.

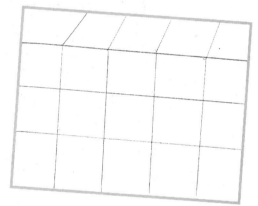

Next, we construct the grid on paper and make a copy for each student. One sheet of paper rarely provides enough note space for major research, so our students expand their charts by taping grids together. It's common to find five or six sheets taped together before the research process is finished. We like this taping process because it allows students to vary the grids to accommodate projects of any size.

A fifth-grade student works on a note-taking grid for a major research project.

The Best Research Reports Ever *Scholastic Professional Books, 1998*

MODELING: Note-Taking With a Research Grid

We begin by displaying a copy of the grid on the overhead projector. We have written the title of our research topic, "Helen Keller," across the top. We show students that the first column on the left is for our sources, so we write "Resource" on top of that column.

On top of the other columns of boxes we write our research questions. The questions for Helen Keller were: What was her early life like? Who were her teachers? What kind of problems did she have? and What were her successes?

"How do you suppose we choose these research questions?" is one of our favorite lead questions. A question like this stimulates students' thinking and involves them in the process. Through class discussion the students realize that we have done a lot of background reading on our topic. They see that we've immersed ourselves in the topic to determine the important aspects of Helen Keller's life. And we show them all of our references.

As we share our references, we show students how we turn the headings in books into questions. We ask students to look at the first word of our questions. They'll say, "Oh, you used the who, what, why, when, where, and how words." We remind students that we might think of other questions as we continue our research and that we can add them to our note-taking grid as we go along.

Helen Keller	What was her early life like?	Who were her teachers?	What kind of problems did she have?	What were her successes?
Resources Young Helen Keller Carol Dresler Educational Reading Services, NJ 1976		- mother - Anne Sullivan	- sick when a baby - temper tantrums	- wrote a book - helped the deaf and blind
Microsoft ENCARTA 1994	- began special education at 7	Anne Sullivan worked with Helen when she was 7. - Macy - Perkins Institute	- got sick when she was 19 months	- learned Braille

The Best Research Reports Ever *Scholastic Professional Books, 1998*

Next, we model how we take notes and organize them on our grid. In the first box in the Resource column, we write the title of one of our references, its author and publisher, the city where it was published, and its copyright date. We explain to our students that we'll use this information later to compile the bibliography.

> *Taking notes on a note-taking grid is successful for all types of research projects, from oral reports to writing raps to writing a major research paper.*

Now, just as with the note-taking mini-lesson, we begin by reading aloud a paragraph from the first reference. We ask, "What information about Helen Keller do we find in this paragraph?" Students realize that the paragraph tells all about her education at home. Together, we decide what our notes will be and write them in the box directly under the question "How did she get her education?" We display another transparency with a paragraph about Helen's tutors and write the notes in the first box under the question about her teachers. All information from our first reference is written in the first row. The third transparency shows an excerpt from another reference. We write the title, author, and so on, of the book in the second box in the left-hand column. Any notes we take from that book go in the second row. We continue modeling until we're certain that our students understand the concept. The students realize that not every box in the grid will be filled. For example, one of our books didn't have any information about Helen Keller's early life, so the box under the question about that is blank.

PRACTICE: Using Research Grids

As students begin their own research, we become encouragers and coaches, giving help as needed. We assist by

Laura uses her research grid to prepare for an oral report on the Chinese calendar.

reading difficult passages aloud, help by locating other references, and work closely with students on a one-on-one basis. "Wow, look at all the information I have on my person" or "I need to find another book because I still don't have much information about her family" are typical comments we hear as students take notes on their topics. The room bubbles with excited tones as the students work; they are fully engaged in the process. Taking notes on a note-taking grid is successful for all types of research projects, from oral reports to writing raps to producing a

The Best Research Reports Ever *Scholastic Professional Books, 1998*

major research paper. What we and our students like about a note-taking grid is that all the like information is grouped together—the notes in one column answer the question at the top.

AUTHENTIC PROJECTS

We never have the students take notes just to learn how to take notes. Before they begin their research and the note-taking process, we discuss the project that they'll use their notes to complete. We want the projects to be authentic, to have a purpose.

Oral Reports

The first projects we have our students present are oral reports using their notes. This is a good way to begin, because the reports are short, and students don't have the task of working through the writing

Ayesha looks at her notes as she presents her oral report on Chinese sculpture and pottery.

process as they would for a written report. As students prepare for their oral reports, we help them make certain they have enough information. They may have to go back and do more research, or maybe they'll have to throw out a question because they simply cannot find any information that answers that question. Then, because their notes are not necessarily in sequential order, the students reorganize the topics they've covered in the most logical order. For example, they probably want to talk about Helen Keller's childhood, education, and teachers before sharing information about her successes. Before giving the oral report, students partner up with a buddy and practice, looking at their notes as necessary.

Interviews

Interviewing is another way to share notes without any writing. Our students like to pretend that they are the person they're researching and that they're being interviewed on radio or television. A table and a pretend microphone are the only props they need. Sometimes students even dress the part. The students make a copy of their research questions and give it to the classmate who's doing the interview. The interviewer asks the questions and the celebrity responds with the information from her notes. Students usually work with partners and exchange roles so that each partner gets to be the interviewer and the interviewee. The partners practice together before the interview begins. (For a mini-lesson on how to interview, see page 49).

The Best Research Reports Ever *Scholastic Professional Books, 1998*

Raps

Raps are another engaging way for students to present research information. After reading and listening to a collection of raps that we found in various magazines, a class of fourth-grade students decided to write raps to share their information about famous Colorado explorers. Each student did research on one explorer and prepared a note-taking grid; then, they were ready to write their raps.

The boys who wrote this rap about the Bent brothers dressed for their presentation as they thought the Bent brothers would have looked. Their rap, costume, and oral expression brought the house down.

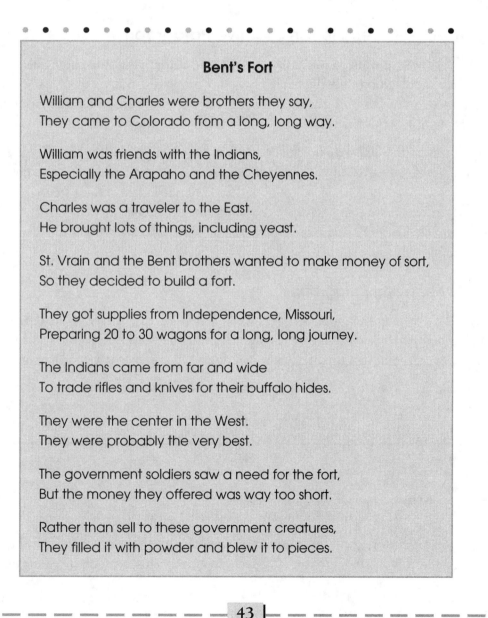

Bent's Fort

William and Charles were brothers they say,
They came to Colorado from a long, long way.

William was friends with the Indians,
Especially the Arapaho and the Cheyennes.

Charles was a traveler to the East.
He brought lots of things, including yeast.

St. Vrain and the Bent brothers wanted to make money of sort,
So they decided to build a fort.

They got supplies from Independence, Missouri,
Preparing 20 to 30 wagons for a long, long journey.

The Indians came from far and wide
To trade rifles and knives for their buffalo hides.

They were the center in the West.
They were probably the very best.

The government soldiers saw a need for the fort,
But the money they offered was way too short.

Rather than sell to these government creatures,
They filled it with powder and blew it to pieces.

The Best Research Reports Ever *Scholastic Professional Books, 1998*

Mini-Lesson: Putting Notes into Text

OBJECTIVE:

To use notes to write effective paragraphs.

Once students have had practice with using note-taking grids to research their oral presentations, they're ready to learn about doing research for report writing. Before they begin, we teach the process of writing a paragraph. It's impossible to overteach this process; students need to practice deciding on the topic sentence and supporting sentences many times before they truly understand the concept.

Getting Started—Criteria for an Effective Paragraph

We locate paragraphs we want to use as examples and put them on transparencies. There are many wonderful nonfiction books available to use for modeling, but we always try to choose samples that relate to our unit of study. For example, when we were studying marine life, we chose this paragraph about the whale's tail from Seymour Simon's *Whales*:

> *A whale has a tail with horizontal flukes, which are different from the vertical tail fins of a fish. The fins of a fish have bones and move from side to side. Flukes have no bones and are moved up and down by powerful muscles connected to the whale's spine. The upward stroke of the tail pushes the whale through the water, sometimes at speeds of more than thirty miles per hour. From tip to tip, the flukes of a great whale are longer than a tall person.*

MODELING: Analyzing Paragraphs

We first read the paragraph to students so they can just enjoy the beauty of the language. After discussing the paragraph, we put the transparency on the overhead projector and again read it aloud. Then we focus on the structure, asking students what makes it a good paragraph.

As students talk, we write their ideas—not their exact words—on chart paper. For example:

Mary: It has one topic. It is all about the tail of a whale.
Joe: Paragraphs need a topic sentence. He compares the tail of a whale
        and the tail of a fish in his topic sentence.
Aaron: He has three supporting ideas in the paragraph.
Season: Upward stroke and tip to tip are examples of vivid words.
Alex: I think the sentences are in order; he doesn't jump all over.

We continue this procedure, putting another transparency on the overhead. Soon the students have generated their own criteria for an effective paragraph. This is much more meaningful

and memorable than if we had just presented them with a list. After discussing several paragraphs, our chart looks like this:

An Effective Paragraph Criteria Chart

- has one topic.
- has a topic sentence.
- has supporting sentences that give details or facts about the topic.
- has vivid words.
- does not have run-on sentences.
- has sentences that make sense and stick to the topic.
- has sentences that are in an order that makes sense.
- has sentences that begin in different ways.
- is made up of sentences that flow.
- is mechanically correct—spelling, punctuation, capitalization, indentation.

We post this chart and also give a copy to each student to refer to later.

Writing Paragraphs

Next, we model for students how to use their summary notes to create well-written, interesting paragraphs. The notes about how whales breathe from the note-taking mini-lesson (page 34) work well for this lesson. You can also take the notes from a student's note-taking grid and model how all the notes under one question can be assembled in a well-written paragraph.

How do whales breathe?

- fish breathe through gills
- whales breathe through lungs
- whales surface to inhale
- nostrils are blowholes
- humpbacks have two blowholes

We begin by reading aloud the notes and then using the think-aloud method. We say, "The topic of this paragraph is about how whales breathe. I want my topic sentence to be the first sentence in the paragraph and to state the main idea of the paragraph. Let's see, 'Whales breathe through their lungs.' That sounds like a good topic sentence. So I'll write it as my first sentence. Now I can refer to my notes and see what supporting facts I can include that explain the topic sentence." We continue thinking aloud and writing until we've written a complete paragraph.

The Best Research Reports Ever *Scholastic Professional Books, 1998*

> Whales breathe through their lungs. Fish breathe through gills. Whales have to come to the surface to inhale. Whales have nostrils; they are called blow-holes. A humpback whale has two blowholes. Most whales have only one.

Students learn a great deal about using notes to write paragraphs as they listen to you think aloud.

Revising a Paragraph

After finishing the draft of the paragraph and writing it on chart paper, it's time to model the revision process for students. We read aloud the paragraph we've written. Students refer to their Effective Paragraph Criteria Chart to help with the revision. They immediately pick up that the paragraph is full of choppy sentences, so it doesn't flow. Together, we figure out how to combine the first two sentences to read "Whales breathe through lungs, while fish breathe through their gills." Another student asks if we can combine the sentences about the nostrils and blowholes since they refer to each other. So we write "Whales have nostrils; they are called blowholes." We try several other changes that we reject because they don't make the paragraph sound any better. Finally, we agree that we have an effective paragraph:

> Whales breathe through their lungs, while fish breathe through gills. Whales have to come to the surface to inhale. Whales have nostrils; they are called blowholes. A humpback whale has two blowholes. Most whales have only one.

PRACTICE: Writing a First Draft

Now it's time for students to use their summary notes on their note-taking grid to write the first draft of a paragraph. If a student has researched and taken notes on several facets of a topic, we encourage him to write several paragraphs. We have our students put aside the reference books and use only their notes. Since students have immersed themselves in their topics and are now knowledgeable about them, they don't have trouble writing in their own words.

Several fifth-grade students are using their note-taking grids as they write their first drafts.

The Best Research Reports Ever *Scholastic Professional Books, 1998*

Conferring and Revising

After students revise their own first drafts, they confer with a peer. The authors take turns reading their drafts and having their partners tell what they like about their work. We all like to hear positive comments, so we encourage our students to always find something positive to say. Then students use the criteria on the Effective Paragraph Criteria Chart (page 45) to guide their discussion. They check for a main idea. Are there supporting details? Do all the sentences refer to the main topic? Partners help each other by making suggestions about sentence structure and style. We encourage them to ask questions when they don't understand something in their partner's paragraph. When they've finished conferring, the two students revise their paragraphs.

Partners Aaron and Emily work together to revise the first drafts of their reports.

As they write, students can refer to the their copies of the Effective Paragraph Chart and the following Revision Checklist.

Revision Checklist

Did I... • refer to my notes and develop my ideas into paragraphs?

• revise my drafts?

• confer with others in writing conferences?

• continue to revise after a conference?

• use a dictionary and thesaurus?

• edit my work so that others can read it?

• correct spelling, punctuation, and grammatical errors?

→

Does my writing show...
- paragraphs built around a main idea?
- the use of supporting ideas for the main idea in each paragraph?
- complete sentences?
- a variety of sentence types that flow?
- appropriate vocabulary?
- consistent use of the correct tense?
- correct spelling?
- correct punctuation?
- agreement between subject and verb?
- agreement between pronoun and antecedent?

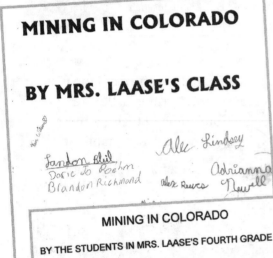

MINING IN COLORADO

BY MRS. LAASE'S CLASS

Landon Bluil
Dorie Jo Roehm
Brandon Richmond
Alee Lindsey
Alex Reeves
Adrianna Newell

MINING IN COLORADO
BY THE STUDENTS IN MRS. LAASE'S FOURTH GRADE

TRAILS

The main trails that the miners used were the Oregon and Santa Fe trails. Later on the miners made two new trails, the Republican and Smokey Hill. Why do you think they called them the Smokey Hill Trail and the Republican Trail? Why, because they go by rivers called the Republican and Smokey Hill. Some of the trails were just for stage coaches.

RANSPORTATION

...lled by oxen or horses. It was not ...el because there were many Indian raids ...agons were damaged and gave way.

...ed to the donkey and were able to carry ... They called the burro the rocky mountain ...ad a bad heehaw voice.

The stage coaches were used for lots of things. The stage coaches carried mail, passengers, supplies, and other things. Stage coaches were pulled by oxen or horses. Sometimes the stage coaches got held up.

The cover and first page of a class book that provided fourth graders with practice in researching and writing, without the task of preparing their own complete report.

AN AUTHENTIC PROJECT:
Class-Authored Book

Writing a class report or book is a good way to get students started researching and writing. It gives them the chance to practice their expertise on writing effective paragraphs for a real purpose, yet they don't have to worry about having their paragraphs flow smoothly from one to another. Titles or headings for the various sections take care of that.

Since we haven't yet modeled or practiced transitions, we don't expect to see that detail in our students' reports. Writing transition sentences or paragraphs is material for another mini-lesson.

For this project we divide the class into small groups of two or three. Each group has a question to answer that relates to a general research topic drawn from a current unit of study. One class authored a book called "Mining in Colorado." Since the students were well into the study of the mining era in Colorado when they began the project, they had the background knowledge needed to begin their research.

First, we have the students brainstorm to generate topics about the mining era. Next, each group chooses one of the topics and turns it into a research question. For example: Who were the famous prospectors? What form of transportation did the miners use? Why were mining towns important? What mining process did the miners use? Then each group goes through the process of taking notes and writing a paragraph or more about their topic. We make sure that the groups give their topics titles so the report will flow smoothly without transitional sentences or paragraphs when we combine the material.

Jay researches a topic with two of his classmates.

When it is time to revise, the groups switch drafts. They use editing pencils or markers—they love using red—to revise. We encourage them to discuss the papers and ask each other questions to clarify confusion before they mark possible changes. After at least two revisions, and final editing by the authors, the class report is ready for publication. Each group keys its section into the computer. For younger children, we may key in the writing. After a student designs a cover, the pages are ready to assemble into a class book. Through this book, our students have practiced taking notes, writing drafts, and editing.

• • • • • • • • • •

Mini-Lesson: Learning to Interview

OBJECTIVE:

To help students conduct an interview and use the information from the interview.

> A Travel Through the Life of Alex Statler
> By Adrienne
> It all started when Alex Jordan Statler was born. This wonderful thing happened April 25, 1986. Alex has a twin named Max. She says, "He is a big pain, but he is my twin." She also has an older brother named Eric who is 11 years old. Alex thinks that he is a pain too.

As Adrienne's profile of Alex shows, interviewing people is a valuable technique for obtaining information from a primary source for reports or other research projects. Our students can get current information from their parents, grandparents, or business people in the community. They can also interview people by telephone or on-line. Stories obtained through an interview can be wonderful additions to a report.

When they interview, our students are actively involved in the process of collecting information. They are practicing all the skills they've been learning—organizing, thinking, listening, speaking, note-taking, and processing information.

Getting Started—Collect Interviews and Stage One

Most middle school students have had some experience with interviewing, but about all elementary students have to say when we ask what they know about interviews is, "You ask someone questions." To help students learn what makes an effective interview, we bring in lots of written interviews that we've collected over time. Sports magazines, movie magazines, and student magazines are excellent sources. Our local newspaper frequently carries interviews of local celebrities as well as a weekly interview with a high school student. Once, the paper featured an interview with a senior citizen volunteer who'd been a frequent visitor to our class. The students really connected to that article. If the interviewee is someone the students know or have heard of, they take a greater interest in the interview. We also videotape interviews from television, giving the students a chance to actually see and hear the interview process.

We tried having students read the interviews to determine the questions the interviewer asked, but we found that most of them couldn't do this. Instead, we realized, students need to see and hear an effective interview in action. So we stage one.

We invite someone to come to the classroom to be interviewed. It may be an administrator, a custodian or cook, a willing parent, or a professional in the community. The possibilities are endless. In advance, we determine and write the questions—20 or more—that we want to ask. We make these into a transparency so that students can see them.

Two middle school students interview each other for the class newspaper.

MODELING: Preparing for the Interview

We show our students the transparency with the questions we've planned for our staged interview and ask, "Why do you suppose we left so much space between each question?" We want the students to see that we leave space for the answers to our questions. After the interview we'll discuss the types of questions we asked. But beforehand, we want our students to see how important it is to plan and prepare for the interview.

Besides having our questions ready, we prepare a hard surface for writing. A clipboard is ideal, but not all students will have clipboards, so we use a magazine and a large paper clip to hold the page of questions to the magazine. We don't use a tape recorder for this first interview because we think that students have enough to handle with just their questions, pencils, and paper. Later, however, we may demonstrate how to conduct an interview using a tape recorder.

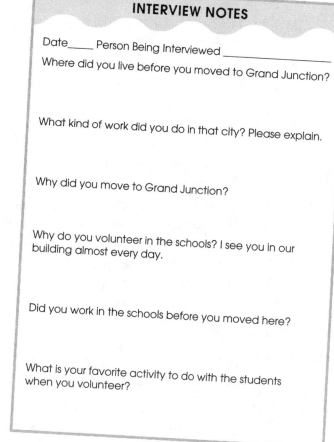

INTERVIEW NOTES

Date_____ Person Being Interviewed _____

Where did you live before you moved to Grand Junction?

What kind of work did you do in that city? Please explain.

Why did you move to Grand Junction?

Why do you volunteer in the schools? I see you in our building almost every day.

Did you work in the schools before you moved here?

What is your favorite activity to do with the students when you volunteer?

Conducting the Interview

As we model an interview with Mr. Mc, a retired scientist, our beginning dialogue sounds something like this:

Mrs. L: Good morning, Mr Mc. I am so glad that I'll be able to interview you this morning. I know how busy you are with all of your volunteer work in the community.

Mr. Mc: I enjoy coming to classrooms and working with the boys and girls. I understand that you're learning how to interview.

Mrs. L: Yes, you are our model. The students will watch us as we work together. Is it all right if I take notes?

Our students observe the question-and-answer procedure as we continue the interview. The questions are on the overhead projector so they can follow along. Students see how we write the answers and how sometimes we deviate from our planned questions because an interesting answer triggers a question we hadn't prepared.

The Best Research Reports Ever *Scholastic Professional Books, 1998*

Mrs. L: I understand you're new to this city; where did you live before?

Mr. Mc: We lived in Los Alamos, which is a city in New Mexico.

Mrs. L: What did you do there?

Mr. Mc: I was a physicist at the National Laboratory.

Mrs. L: Could you tell me about the work that you did?

Mr. Mc: I did all kinds of experiments and worked on big projects. I have lots of pictures showing what I did. Perhaps I could bring them into the classroom and explain my work through pictures.

Mrs. L: That would be great. What brought you to our city?

Mr. Mc: I retired and decided to leave New Mexico. I like it here.

Mrs. L: Why do you volunteer in the schools?

Mr. Mc: I like working with students. I never had time before. Now I feel like it's payback time. I want to pay back to the community for all the things that the community gave to me.

Mrs. L: That is wonderful. What kind of things do you do in the schools?

(the interview continues)

When the interview is over and the subject of the interview is gone, we ask students what they saw and heard. The dialogue goes something like this:

S: Sometimes you skipped questions.

T: Yes, sometimes the questions I had prepared didn't work out. Sometimes an answer prompted a question that I hadn't thought of before.

S: You were polite.

T: I'm glad you noticed that. I always try to be polite.

T: Look at the beginning word of many of my questions. What do you notice?

S: Oh, most of your questions begin with the question words—who, what, why, when, where, and how.

T: Good. When you're preparing your questions you'll want to think of the W-H words. You can learn a lot when your questions begin with those words. Did you notice that I didn't ask any questions that could be answered by just the words yes or no? Why do you think I avoided yes and no questions?

S: You don't get much information from a yes or a no.

T: How did I look? What was my body language?

S: You looked at the person. You looked like you were interested.

After our conversation, the students help develop a chart that will guide them when they interview.

Including Quotations in Interviews

After the model interview, we show our students how a direct quotation from the interviewee adds to an article or report. We copy onto a transparency a section with a quotation from one of our sample interviews. We observe how the quotation adds to the write-up. We also review the rules for punctuating quotations. Whenever our students use an interview as a reference, we remind them to include at least one direct quote in the text.

Using the Interview Material

If the interview is one of several reference sources a student will use for a report or other project, he adds the information to the note-taking grid. Sometimes our students write up the interview information as an article for a class newspaper or to prepare an oral report. If that's the case, the students can work directly from their question-and-answer notes.

PROFILES
Fourth Grade Students
Wingate Elementary

April 22, 1996   Grand Junction, Colorado   Special Edition

Ryon Hart
By Tyler Thrasher

I have someone for you to meet. His name is Ryon Hart. He was born in Puerto Rico in 1986. At the age of 7, he moved to the United States.

His family members are: Marina, his sister, is in fifth grade, his dad, Alec, owns 13 restaurants, 11 of them are in Puerto Rico, and his mom Norie, who helps us at school a lot.

Ryon says when he grow up he wants to be a soccer player and marine biologist. He would like to be a marine biologist when he retires from soccer.

Ryon says that his favorite tv show is the Discovery channel. He likes it because he says that he can learn interesting facts.

Ryon says his favorite animals are a cheetah and a gibbon. They are interesting animals.

Ryon like to collect marbles and pennies by date. I wonder how many marbles he has?

Some of Ryon's hobbies are playing soccer and climbing trees. It sounds like fun.

Ryon is at an interesting age, he is nine years old and his favorite subject is math because he likes to count and have fun with numbers. It sounds like Ryon has a fun life.

The Best Research Reports Ever   Scholastic Professional Books, 1998

AN AUTHENTIC PROJECT: Classroom Profiles

After reading an interview in our local newspaper with the scientist who had spent many volunteer hours in our classroom, our students were very excited and were immediately turned on to the idea of doing their own interviews. They decided they wanted to interview each other and make their own newspaper. It was a great way for them to perfect their interviewing skills—skills that they can use to bring life to other research projects. Their prior knowledge and enthusiasm had given them a purpose for learning how to interview.

To begin this project, we pair our students for the interviews. The students prepare their questions, tailoring them to fit their partners and the information they need. With interview questions and pencils in hand they begin the interview process. We float from group to group, interacting as needed.

Whenever students use an interview as a reference, we remind them to include at least one direct quote in the text.

After the pairs have interviewed each other, the writing process begins. We've had many lessons on writing a dynamic lead sentence, so a reminder is all that's needed for most of the students. But we reteach or assist those students who still need help.

After students have finished their first drafts, they confer with their partners to check for accuracy. Frequently we hear, "But that *is* what I heard you say" or "No, I meant to say..." Once the information is correct, they revise and edit.

We or our students input the interviews into the computer in column format just like a newspaper. Our class photographer is responsible for taking individual pictures of the students. When it's time to publish, the students take the photos and a printout of each interview article and lay out the paper. You can scan the photos if you have the equipment. We use the cut-and-tape method. It's an exciting day when the newspaper comes off the school copy machine.

Mini-Lesson: Learning Log Responses

OBJECTIVE:

To encourage student writing and learning in content areas and to reflect on what they're learning.

> Prehistoric People Puzzle
>
> There is a huge puzzle being put together. The puzzle's picture is of the prehistoric people that lived hundreds of years ago. The people that are putting the puzzle together are called archaeologists. They spend their days digging up things that prehistoric people left behind. Things they left behind are pottery, jars, jewelry, and things like that. These are the pieces of the puzzle.
>
> Nobody knows why the Anasazi Indians left their beautiful homes but still I wonder why they did. I also wonder if the Anasazi and Utes were enemies and how they wove yucca into things.   —Learning Log Response
>   Michelle, Fourth Grade

Through learning logs—notebooks in which students write their thoughts about what they're learning in the content areas—our students get the practice they need to reflect on the research information they've gathered. To use research for reports or other original projects, students need to be able to write more than just the facts. They need to ask questions, make connections, analyze the various points of view of the authors, and express their own emotions. Learning logs help students actively respond to what they're learning. In their logs, they reflect on their experiences, assess what makes sense and what doesn't, and record their thoughts and feelings.

> *Through learning logs, students learn to question and seek answers.*

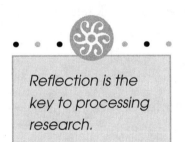

> *Reflection is the key to processing research.*

Getting Started—A Notebook for Each Student

Each student needs a notebook. A spiral or composition notebook works fine. We recommend a single subject notebook. Students keep their notebooks in their desks so they are readily accessible.

MODELING

Students don't automatically know how to respond in a learning log. They need on-the-job training. We can't complete this training in one day or one week; it extends over time. Since the format for learning log responses can vary, depending on the purpose, we ask our students to respond in different ways. And each time we ask for a different kind of response, we model what we're expecting by thinking aloud as we go through the process.

A Modeled Response

We wrote the following modeled response on a transparency after our students attended an assembly program presented by a mountain man. We were thinking aloud about the assembly

and about what we wanted to write. We made sure that students understood that they were hearing us think.

Directions to the class:
> *I am going to write a response in my learning log about the mountain man assembly. It may sound like I am talking to myself, but I want you to hear what I am thinking as I figure out what I want to write about the assembly. I am going to write my response on this transparency so you can read what I write.*

Teacher thinking aloud:
> *I really liked the assembly so I will start out writing a statement about that.*

Written text:
> What a tremendous assembly. (All written text is read aloud as it is being written.)

Teacher thinking aloud:
> *I need to tell what the assembly was about.*

Written text:
> Mr. Johnson pretended that he was a real mountain man. He really did look like one.

Teacher thinking aloud:
> *I can't just say he looked like a mountain man. I need to describe how he looked.*

Written text:
> His clothes were made out of animal hides. He said that he made his clothes. His pants and shirt took three deer hides. It didn't look like it would take that many.

Teacher thinking aloud:
> *I just gave my own opinion. I reflected on what I saw. Now I want to tell about trapping beaver.*

Written text:
> He told us about trapping beaver. He sold the beaver skins so people in New York could make top hats. He also showed us lots of different animal skins.

Teacher thinking aloud:
> *I liked the tall tale at the end but I don't want to retell the whole story, so I will just mention how funny it was.*

Written text:
> The best part of the assembly was the tall tale that he told at the end. We all laughed and laughed.

Teacher thinking aloud:
> *I don't think I could have lived in the mountains back then. That is a good way to end my response, I will write an "I wonder" sentence.*

Written text:

I wonder if I could have lived in the mountains like the real mountain men did.

After we discuss what students heard us doing and we respond to any concerns, students write their own responses to the presentation. We encourage them to express their own thoughts. What we liked and learned may not be what they liked or learned.

Another Modeled Response

As a culminating science activity, we ask students to summarize in their learning logs what they learned about eye placement and the eating habits of dinosaurs. Again we model a response before we ask the students to write their own.

Directions to the class:

I want you to summarize in your learning logs what you have learned about the importance of eye placement on a dinosaur's head. Before you write, however, I want to model a response for you. I want you to listen to what I am thinking as I plan and write my response. It is important that you think and plan before your write.

Teacher thinking aloud:

We have been studying about dinosaur eyes. We really did some neat experiments, but I am not going to write about those. I am going to write about what scientists have discovered about their eyes.

Written text: (The following paragraph is read aloud as it is being written.)

Scientists have discovered that dinosaurs either had their eyes in the front of their heads or more to the sides. The dinosaurs who had their eyes in the front were meat eaters. They were predators who were looking ahead for their next meal. The dinosaurs who had their eyes on the sides of their heads were plant eaters. They were always watching out for the predators while they ate grass.

Teacher thinking aloud:

I need to reread what I wrote. I want to make certain I included enough details. Oh, I see I forgot to say that the grass eaters are called prey because they were meals for the predators.

Written text:

These dinosaurs were called prey because they were meals for the predators.

Modeling does pay off. Students know what is expected. We are providing them with on-the-job training.

The Best Research Reports Ever *Scholastic Professional Books, 1998*

Reflecting

We pay particular attention to helping our students learn to reflect on what they're learning, because it takes time to develop that skill. We have our classes begin with oral reflections. After students are comfortable with these, they move naturally into writing their reflections and incorporating them into their learning log summaries.

ACTIVITIES: Oral Reflection Activities

- After completing a read-aloud book, reflect, as a class, on the book—opinions about the writing and content, the author's point of view, how the pictures influence our ideas, and so on.

- After a science experiment, reflect on the results of the experiment. Discuss what the results might have been if different substances had been used.

Sample of a student's learning log response about John Adams for a social studies unit on the American Revolution.

- Reflect on how a woman might have felt as she traveled west in a covered wagon.

Different Ways to Respond in a Learning Log

- *Summarize what you learned.* After a particular lesson, students combine information, select what's important, and condense data to make it their own.

- *Ask questions about things you don't understand.* After a science experiment, math class, video, assembly, or field trip, for example, students reflect on what they still don't understand.

- *Brainstorm what you already know about the topic.* Students delve into their background knowledge, similar to the K in a KWL chart (See page 9).

- *Generate questions before we start the unit.* Students ponder what they'd like to learn, similar to the W in the KWL chart.

- *Predict what the video, observation, experiment, or experience will cover.* Using predicting skills, students connect new ideas to prior knowledge and become active learners.

- *Choose a person from a historical era and write diary entries as that person.* To take on the role of another person, students have to do a great deal of reflecting.

The Best Research Reports Ever *Scholastic Professional Books, 1998*

• *Take notes while other students are presenting reports and explain what they learned.* This is a powerful tool to help students focus on their classmates' presentations and learn about the material their peers have researched. This almost guarantees an attentive audience.

Learning Log Starters

Critical thinking becomes automatic when you ask students to write regularly in different ways. We frequently provide our students with learning log starters. We post the following list from the *Colorado Communicator* (June 1996, Colorado Council of the International Reading Association).

Students summarize what they learned and reflect on it in their learning logs.

Nonfiction Starters

I learned...	I never knew...
I already knew that...	I was wrong to think...
I wonder why...	I still don't know...
An important date is ...	I learned how to...
The confusing thing is ...	This helped me explain...
I was surprised...	I also want to read...
The index helped me...	I would recommend this book to...
I like learning...	I would like to share my learning by...
Some interesting facts are...	This book answered my questions about...
I want to learn more about...	

Now that students have gained basic research skills and practiced them on activities that don't require writing or that require writing only short paragraphs, they can go on to bigger projects without feeling overwhelmed. The next chapter will show how we guide students through the process of preparing a complete report, including examples of targeted practice projects. Of course, we continually repeat our skills mini-lessons for students who need them.

Making a Molehill Out of a Mountain: The 100% Successful Research Paper

> I am proud of my report, "Holidays in China." It was not hard to write because the note-taking grid made writing notes to answer my questions easy. The outline helped me know the order to put my information in, and I learned how to truly revise and edit. It was fun learning about the holidays and festivals in China.
>
> —*Sarah, Fifth Grade*

Something magical and wonderful happens in a lively classroom where inquiry is important, where students have choice in their topics, and where they receive the instruction they need to conduct their research. We've found that after our students have had several experiences with note-taking for research projects such as oral presentations, they're confident and ready to write reports. They're eager to explore topics of their choice within a unit of study or topics they've become curious about on their own. They can see a purpose for their learning and, as a result, assume more responsibility in the research process.

> ## Stages of Report Writing
>
> Generate ideas
>
> Choose a topic
>
> Create a list of questions the report will answer
>
> Gather information
>
>   Locate resources
>
>   Write notes
>
> Write drafts (could be several)
>
> Revise drafts
>
> Edit final drafts
>
> Publish report
>
> Evaluate

Generating Ideas for Research Topics

Before students choose topics to research for a unit of study, we immerse them in the unit for a while, giving them time to read and explore it so they can formulate questions that are important to them and that may provide them with a report topic. We do this in several ways. First, as a new unit of study begins to unfold, we invite our students to visit a related interest center. We fill the center with books and other print materials, pictures, artifacts, music, videos, and anything else that may intrigue them. As students explore the items and skim or read the printed materials, they start to wonder and ask questions.

We also read aloud to the students and discuss the new information with them to generate questions. As students think of questions or topics they want to investigate, they jot them down in their learning logs.

The KWL strategy is another successful technique we use to get students involved in generating questions about a new unit of study. We divide a large sheet of paper into sections labeled (K) What We Already Know, (W) What We Want to Find Out, and (L) What We Learned and Still Want to

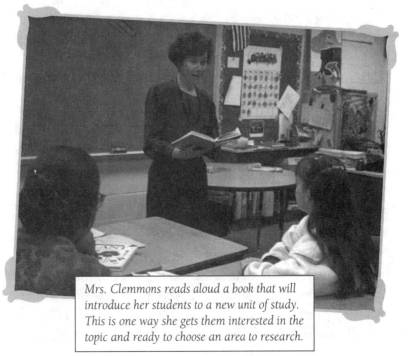

Mrs. Clemmons reads aloud a book that will introduce her students to a new unit of study. This is one way she gets them interested in the topic and ready to choose an area to research.

The Best Research Reports Ever *Scholastic Professional Books, 1998*

A group of students brainstorm for questions they have about a new unit of study.

Learn. As students tell us what they already know about the topic and what they want to find out, we write their responses in the K and W sections. Throughout our study of the unit, we and the students record new concepts learned and additional questions generated by the new knowledge in the L section. We like to use this activity with the entire class because the responses of one child may help another generate ideas. However, as a variation, we sometimes give our students their own copies of the chart and ask them to record their ideas independently.

Another way to get students to think critically about what they want to learn is to have them sit in small groups and brainstorm questions they have about the unit of study. One student records the questions, and each learner writes in his learning log questions or topics he might be excited about exploring.

Sometimes we want students to do research reports that are not related to a unit of study. They conduct their inquiry on topics they're personally curious about and would like to explore. We help them think of topics by giving them time to stop and think and record in their learning logs questions they can hardly wait to investigate. During a class discussion, we invite students to share their questions as an additional way to help generate ideas for others.

Choosing a Research Topic and Making It Specific

After students have been immersed in the unit for a while, we ask them to reflect on the questions or topics listed on the KWL chart or in their learning logs to choose something they have a real desire to research. We encourage them to choose an interesting topic they really care about—one they have a burning desire to investigate that is just jumping out at them and saying, "Choose me!"

We remind students to choose a specific topic. We explain that if the topic is too narrow, there may not be enough information to write a report, but if it's too broad, there may be too much information for one report. If a student selects a topic that's too narrow, we discuss ways he may broaden it. Topics that are too narrow often arise as a result of student questions that have a yes or no answer. These questions can be reworded to encompass more details. For example, Andrea wanted to find out if the children in ancient Egypt went to school. After discussing this question with us and exploring other related ideas she was wondering about, she decided her

topic for research would be How the Children in Ancient Egypt Were Educated.

More often, a student chooses a topic that is too broad, such as sports. Sometimes, to help a student make his topic more specific, we have him create a web by placing the large topic in the center of the paper with categories and subtopics branching out from it. For example, when Kevin made the following web on sports, he discovered he was most interested in researching ice hockey.

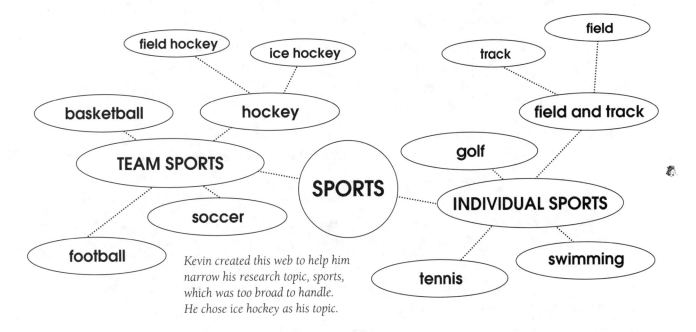

Kevin created this web to help him narrow his research topic, sports, which was too broad to handle. He chose ice hockey as his topic.

Lauren chose animals in China as a topic, but she couldn't make a web because she didn't know which animals lived in China. In this case, we suggested that Lauren look in one of the references about China to find the kinds of animals living there. Using the computer and a CD-ROM, she was excited to discover the names of about forty animals in China. She decided she would love to research the giant panda because it looks so cute and cuddly. When asked what she already knew about pandas, she only knew they live in China, eat bamboo, and are black and white. Asking students to list what they know about their topics before they begin their research helps them to connect the new knowledge they'll be acquiring to concepts they already know.

> *Asking students to list information they already know about their topics helps them to connect the new knowledge they will be learning in their research to concepts they already know.*

The Best Research Reports Ever *Scholastic Professional Books, 1998*

Listing Specific Questions the Report Will Answer

Once our students have chosen their topics for research, we ask them to list specific questions they're wondering about and want their reports to answer. We encourage them to use open-ended questions or the W-H questions (who, what, when, where, why, and how). We help students who can't come up with questions by asking *them* questions about their subjects. Some learners are helped by the suggestion that they think about their topic and quickly jot down any questions that come to mind. It is vital to have discussions with students about their progress during the planning stages and throughout the research process.

These initial questions will help guide students' reading and note-taking, but they shouldn't be limited to these. As they investigate their subjects, they undoubtedly may think of and add to their list additional questions they want to answer and discuss in their reports. They may want to rewrite or omit some of the original questions.

Lauren listed some of the following questions before she started her research on giant pandas and added some others as they came to mind while she was reading and thinking:

What do pandas look like?	How big are they?
What do they eat? When do they eat?	What do they live in?
When and where do they sleep?	What are they like?
Who are their enemies?	What part of China do they live in?
Which family do they belong to?	How much do pandas weigh?
What are the names of famous pandas?	How many pandas are left in the world today?

While Lauren has a long list, other students may have fewer questions and thus end up with a report with fewer paragraphs than hers.

Gathering Information

Because our students have already had at least two experiences with research prior to the research paper, they're familiar with using a variety of resources and feel comfortable with note-taking. Feeling confident, they approach the task with a great attitude.

Being familiar with research skills makes the process of gathering information for a written report easier for students.

Resources: Even though students have used different resources in prior research, they benefit from a review of how to use the parts of expository texts to find pertinent information and the many sources available to them. (See Chapter Two: Discovering the Tools of the Book, page 18, and Searching for References, page 24.)

It's important that students be required to use a minimum number of resources. The number will depend on the grade level and the research topic. For most research topics, we require at least three sources, only one of which can be an encyclopedia—print or CD-ROM. However, they can certainly use more. We encourage them to use as many resources as they need to answer their questions and to thoroughly investigate their topics.

Note-Taking Grids: Our students use the data retrieval charts, which we call note-taking grids, for writing and organizing their notes. In the first box at the top left-hand side, we have them write "resources." Some students prefer to write "bibliography" instead, because the boxes underneath the heading will contain the information—author, title, city where the book is published, publisher, and copyright date—that they'll use in writing the bibliographies for their reports. This data also helps them refer back to their sources at a later date. In each of the other boxes across the top of the grid, they write one of their questions. If they have more questions than boxes, they may glue or tape together as many grids as needed.

We prefer using the note-taking grids rather than index cards because students don't lose them and the bibliographical information is recorded next to the notes taken from that source. (If you prefer that your students use index cards, you can have them write one question at the top of each card, note the source, and make a separate card for the full information about each resource.) When the grids aren't in use, students keep them in their writing folders. When students have taped two or more grids together, they fold them for storage.

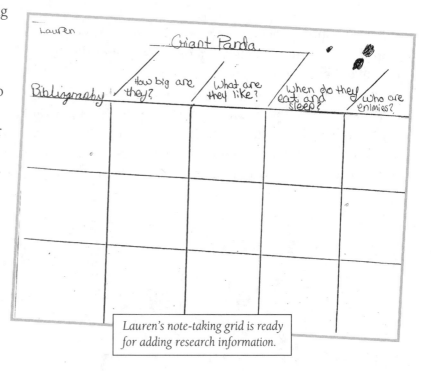

Lauren's note-taking grid is ready for adding research information.

Revisiting Note-Taking Skills: After our students have written their questions on the note-taking grids, we review the mini-lesson on writing notes so that students won't be tempted to copy sentences from the sources unless they want to include them in their reports as a direct quote. (See Chapter Three: Note-Taking Strategies for Text.) After we model how to take notes by writing only the important words, we model how to write a quote by copying the words from text or an interview exactly as they were written or said and placing quotation marks before and after the quote. Students may want to include one relevant quote in their reports,

The Best Research Reports Ever *Scholastic Professional Books, 1998*

but we find they usually don't want more than one. We post charts in the classroom with the criteria for writing notes and quotes.

Doing Daily Self-Evaluations

Now our young researchers are ready, and they're excited about locating their reference materials. But before they begin, we provide them with Self-Evaluation Charts that they will complete at the end of each writing period. By analyzing how they use their time, students develop better work habits. They learn to stay on task and complete assignments on time. We find that they tend to waste much less time when they have to evaluate their accomplishments daily and hand in the charts. On their Self-Evaluation Charts, students note the activity they're working on, what they accomplished, a self-evaluation of their work, and their plans for next time.

Reflecting on how students use their time is beneficial in helping them develop better work habits.

We also include a column on the chart labeled "How can I help you?," where students can request assistance if they're having difficulty. For instance, a student may have looked in several sources for an answer to one of his questions but still can't locate any information. We may be busy helping other students and unaware of his problem. By checking this column on the charts each day, we can plan to give the appropriate assistance the next day. If more than one student needs the same kind of help, we can group students for the necessary instruction.

Name Helen					
Date	Activity	Accomplishments	Self-evaluation	Plans for next time	How can I help you?
Feb 3	Notes	I took notes for almost every question.	I didn't fool around.	Find more information.	Can you help me look more up on the Acropolis and the Parthenon?
Feb 5	Notes	I am almost finished with my notes.	I looked for books with my topic.	To try to finish my notes.	
Feb 10	Notes	I think I am finished with my notes. I planned my story board.	I didn't waste my time and got my work done.	To get on the computer.	
Feb 11	Notes/computer	I finished my Title page and started another. I put my notes in different order so I would know what to write on the pages for my slide show.	I tried to finish my 2nd page on the computer.	To get on the computer to complete at least one more page tomorrow.	

Helen uses her self-evaluation form to monitor her progress.

Writing Notes

We have students do most of their research in school so that we can assist them and so they have access to the classroom and library resources. We also want to encourage their collaboration with other students. The librarian is a great resource, so we coordinate times with her when our students can use the library as well as times when she is available to work with small groups. While some

The Best Research Reports Ever *Scholastic Professional Books, 1998*

students are reading nonfiction books and writing notes, others may be at the computer getting information from the Internet or sending electronic mail to experts in various fields, such as scientists at NASA. We find ourselves busily rotating from student to student in the classroom or library, answering questions and helping students locate material and read passages. At other times, we are reviewing or reteaching needed skills, such as interviewing techniques for the learner who is planning to interview a person as part of his research. (See Chapter Three: Learning to Interview, page 49.) Throughout the note-taking process we are on the lookout for materials students can use in their investigations. We also encourage the researchers to share any information they come across that may be related to a classmate's topic.

Setting Due Dates

After a day of researching, which allows students to become a little more acquainted with their topics, we discuss and mutually agree on a date for the notes to be due. We also set dates for completion of interviews. How much time students will need for note-taking will vary according to the complexity of the research topic, the grade level, and the amount of classroom time scheduled for research. However, we're flexible about due dates. As students work on their research, we may notice that some will need additional time, and we'll revise their due dates.

Rachel and Michelle write notes for their research projects.

In addition to dates for completing notes and interviews, our students have a midpoint date on their calendars on which they'll evaluate what they've accomplished thus far on their note-taking and set goals for completing the notes. The students hand in these evaluations and their notes so that we can also evaluate their progress and confer with them to clarify any uncertainties and make plans to provide any special help they may need. We may revise the due dates again at this point. We want to give students plenty of time to thoroughly investigate their topics and do quality work.

Organizing the Notes

Putting Topics in Order: When students finish writing notes, we have them decide on the order in which they want the topics presented in their reports. We stress that if the report needs to be written in a time sequence, they need to think about what happened first, what happened second, and so on. If the report describes something, we ask them to think about

The Best Research Reports Ever *Scholastic Professional Books, 1998*

the order in which they want to write the description. The topics need to be in a sequence that makes sense and enables the reader to understand them. After studying the questions or topics across the top of the note-taking grid, we ask them to number the top-ics to indicate the most logical order. If your students used note cards, they can arrange these in the order they plan to discuss them in the report.

Outlining: Preparing simple outlines is a great help to stu-dents for organizing their reports. As we explain how to write an outline, we model writing one—using notes we've already written—on a large sheet of paper. We show stu-dents how they can determine the main ideas from the ques-tions or headings on the note-taking grid. We write the main ideas next to Roman numerals, and the supporting details, or notes giving answers to the questions, next to capital letters. We post our model outline for the students to refer to as they write their own.

Lauren's note-taking grid for her report on the giant panda is taking shape.

Sample Outline

Government of Ancient Egypt

I. Type of government
  A. Theocracy
  B. Pharaoh or king was god
  C. Absolute power

II. Government officials
  A. Responsible to the pharaoh
  B. Vizier
  C. Treasurer
  D. Tax collector
  E. Minister of public works
  F. Army commander

III. Provinces
  A. Nomes
  B. Governors
  C. Mayors

IV. Taxes
  A. Goods
  B. Labor

V. Military
  A. Fleet of galley ships
  B. Army of drafted men
  C. Militia in each province
  D. Mercenaries

The Best Research Reports Ever *Scholastic Professional Books, 1998*

Some students may identify a theme or main point in their notes and write their outlines around that theme. Others may find that some of their notes don't belong with a topic and decide to omit them. For example, Lauren had written notes about the red panda but decided to omit them when she wrote her outline because they didn't pertain to the giant panda, the topic on which she'd decided to concentrate.

Students use their notes to write outlines that will guide the order of their finished reports.

After completing the outlines, some students notice that they don't have enough information and will need to do additional research.

Lauren
Giant Pandas

I. What family do they belong to?
  A. Bear
  B. Raccoon
  C. Family of their own

II. Where in China do they live?
  A. North
  B. South

III. Baby pandas
  A. When it is born
  B. Size
  C. Mother

IV. Size
  A. One month
  B. One year
  C. Adult

V. What do they act like?
  A. Sleep
  B. Females
  C. Males
  D. Bad eye sight

VI. What happens when in heat?
  A. Females
  B. Males

VII. What do they eat?
  A. Wild
  B. Zoo

VIII. Who are the enemies?
  A. Snow leopards
  B. Wild dogs

IX. What are some famous pandas?
  A. Ling-Ling and Hsing-Hsing
  B. Han-Han and Mei-Mei
  C. Su-Lin

X. How many are left today?
  A. 600
  B. Need to protect them

Lauren used the notes on her note-taking grid to create this outline, which she'll refer to as she writes her report.

The Best Research Reports Ever *Scholastic Professional Books, 1998*

Developing Criteria for Written Reports

We tell students that before they start writing their reports, we want to discuss what makes a good report. Then we begin a chart that we label "Criteria for Good Report Writing."

The Introductory Paragraph:

> *The great whales are the world's giant animals. This humpback whale is breaching—jumping almost clear out of the water and then crashing down in a huge spray of foam. The humpback whale is longer than a big bus and heavier than a trailer truck. Some great whales are even larger. Just the tongue of a blue whale weighs as much as an elephant....*

After showing a transparency of this passage from Seymour Simon's book, *Whales*, we read it aloud. We explain to students that this is the opening paragraph of the book and ask them why it's a good beginning paragraph. As they contribute ideas, we write their ideas on our chart.

The introductory paragraph
- tells what the report is about.
- is interesting and makes you want to continue reading.
- uses good descriptive words.

Next, we show the first paragraph from *Whales and Sharks and Other Creatures of the Deep* by Susanne Santoro Miller (Simon & Schuster, 1982).

> *Streaks of light slant down through blue-green waters. A dark form slowly passes into view. Suddenly, an echoing cry breaks the underwater silence. The first long high notes are followed by deeper ones. Now a second voice joins in, then a faraway third, repeating the same notes. Over and over, for an hour or more, the sounds continue, like the slow warbles of a robin. This is the music of the humpback whales, and their strange, mysterious song fills the depths.*

After reading this paragraph, students agree that it is a good introduction for a report because it grabbed their attention and contained an interesting, descriptive simile. We add these two criteria to our chart.
- grabs the reader's attention.
- can contain similes.

We explain to students that their reports need a good opening paragraph, but they don't have to write it first. We discuss why it may be easier to write the body of the report before writing the introductory paragraph. Students realize that they may get good ideas for an opening paragraph as they write the body of the report and that even if they do write a first paragraph early on, they may want to change it later.

> *Reports need a good opening paragraph, but students don't have to write it first. It may be easier to write the body of the report first.*

Giant Pandas

Do you know that the giant pandas belong to the bear family? Some people think they are a part of the marsupial family, but they aren't. Some scientists place them in the raccoon family or in a family of their own. They can't agree on how to classify them. I agree with the scientists who say they belong to the bear family.

Niagara Falls
by Laura

Would you want to go down the fast moving Niagara Falls? Most people would say no, but some dare devils would say yes! People used to go over the falls in barrels. Most of the men and women who went over died or got badly hurt. People who wanted to get attention did things other than going over the falls; they walked on a tightrope across the top of the falls. Most normal people wouldn't do that either.

The Great Wall of China

The Great Wall of China is about 2222 years old. It has been added on to over the years, so it has become bigger. Now the Great Wall is 3750 miles long. Ten men could stand side-by-side on the wall, and could all fit. If five men stood on top of each other, you would have the height of the Great Wall.

The Body of the Report: The section of *Whales and Sharks and Other Creatures of the Deep* entitled "Humpback Whales" is a good example of how a report might read. We place a transparency of the entire passage on the screen to help the students identify other criteria that we can add to our chart for good report writing. We also show them some examples of good reports former students have written. On another day we read aloud all of *Whales* by Seymour Simon. With each example, we identify the characteristics of good report writing and place them on our chart.

Because students have been identifying the criteria of good writing in prior writing lessons, they easily identify some of the characteristics related to those lessons, such as writing effective paragraphs (see Chapter Three: Putting Notes Into Text, page 44) for the body of the report. Having the students involved in identifying the criteria and posting the chart they helped develop reminds them of our expectations for good written reports and provides guidelines they can follow while they're writing. A copy of our final chart follows.

Having the students involved in identifying the criteria for good report writing, and posting our chart they helped develop reminds them of our expectations for good written reports and provides guidelines they can follow while they're writing.

Criteria for Good Report Writing

A report needs a good introductory paragraph that
- tells what the report is about.
- grabs the reader's attention.
- is interesting and makes you want to continue reading.
- uses good descriptive words.
- can contain similes.

The body of the report is written in paragraphs. Each paragraph
- is about one topic.
- has a topic sentence.
- contains supporting details.
- has sentences that are needed and are related to the topic.
- contains sentences that are complete and not choppy.
- has clear sentences that make sense.
- has sentences arranged in good order.

The report
- has paragraphs arranged in an understandable order that makes sense.
- contains interesting, vivid vocabulary.
- should be written in my words and sound like me.
- may contain pictures, charts, drawings, and diagrams.
- contains enough information to explain the topic completely.
- is interesting to read.
- has a good closing paragraph with a strong ending statement.
- has a title page and bibliography.
- is typed or written neatly.

The report needs a good concluding paragraph that
- summarizes the main points made in the report.
- lets the reader know the report is finished.

Words are used correctly.
Correct capitalization and punctuation are used.
Words are spelled correctly.

The Best Research Reports Ever   *Scholastic Professional Books, 1998*

Writing Drafts

Katie writes the first draft of her report on recreation in China. She makes sure to leave lines so she'll be able to revise it.

We stress to students that first drafts don't look like the finished pieces of nonfiction writing we've been studying. As we've done in previous lessons, we model writing a paragraph from notes, showing how a paragraph answers a research question. We make sure that we don't write the model perfectly so our students will be able to see how we revise and edit it. (See Chapter Three for more information on putting notes into text.) While drafting, students use their outlines and refer to their notes as needed. If they're not composing their drafts on computers, they skip lines to allow room for revision. We also remind them to refer to the Criteria for Good Report Writing Chart as a guideline.

The Concluding Paragraph: When some of the students approach the end of the first draft, we review in a mini-lesson how to end the report. Following the same procedure we used in the focus lesson about beginning paragraphs, we make a transparency of the last page of *Whales* to show the strong statement Seymour Simon used to end his nonfiction book.

> *Whales are one of the few wild animals that are commonly friendly to humans they encounter. Many people feel that we have an obligation to preserve these intelligent and special animals.*
>
> *Will whales be allowed to remain to share the world with us? The choice is ours.*

After reading *Sharks* by Seymour Simon (HarperCollins, 1995), we study his last paragraph.

> *Sharks have been swimming the oceans for longer than people have even existed. The earliest known sharks lived more than 400 million years ago. That was 200 million years before the first dinosaurs. Rather than thinking of sharks as monsters to be destroyed, we can learn to appreciate their interesting lives. If we understand their behavior, we can avoid most dangerous encounters and live in harmony with these most awesome fish.*

After hearing these endings, the students realize that a report needs a good closing paragraph. They recognize that the conclusion summarizes the main points made in the report and lets the reader know the report is finished. We add these

The conclusion summarizes the main points made in the report and lets the reader know the report is finished.

The Best Research Reports Ever *Scholastic Professional Books, 1998*

statements to our chart, Criteria for Good Report Writing. We stress to students that they are still writing the first drafts of their reports and they may want to revise this final paragraph along with the rest of the piece.

Sharing Successes and Requesting Assistance: During the drafting and revision stages, we set aside about five minutes at the end of writing workshop each day to invite students to share something they've written that they especially like or to discuss an idea they're having

Lauren and Sarah revise their own drafts.

difficulty expressing. Together, we celebrate beautiful phrases and well-written sentences and offer suggestions to those asking for help. We emphasize that we're a community of learners learning from one another. This special time helps create a positive and supportive environment in which students develop confidence in their writing ability and are not afraid to be risk takers.

Revising Drafts

We write first drafts, we tell our students, to get our ideas on paper. We explain that to develop our drafts into final pieces of writing we must revise and revise them to make them understandable and interesting to readers. We sometimes demonstrate that revision takes lots of time by showing students a tall stack of drafts we saved from one of our writing projects.

Working Alone: Upon completion of their first drafts, we ask our students to read their work and check on content. Many students find it beneficial to read their drafts aloud softly to themselves. They also need a checklist to refer to as they revise. We give students copies of the Criteria for Good Report Writing Chart to keep beside them as they revise. Or we give them a related revision checklist such as the following:

The Best Research Reports Ever *Scholastic Professional Books, 1998*

Revision Checklist for Report Writing

Name .... Date ....

.... Is my writing clear when I read it to myself?

.... Does my beginning paragraph grab the reader's attention?

.... Did I organize my report into paragraphs?

.... Did I develop my ideas and support them with specific information?

.... Does all of the information belong?

.... Are my ideas clearly written so that other people can understand what I am saying?

.... Did I use complete sentences?

.... Did I combine some of my short sentences to make longer ones?

.... Are my ideas in each paragraph in a sequence that is clear to another reader?

.... Are my paragraphs in a sequence that is clear and understandable to other readers?

.... Did I include enough details to explain my topic completely and to make my writing clear and interesting to another person?

.... Did I use interesting, vivid vocabulary?

.... Do I have a good closing paragraph and ending statement?

The Best Research Reports Ever *Scholastic Professional Books, 1998*

Getting Mini-Lesson Help During Revision: To aid the students in revision, we read their drafts and then focus mini-lessons on needed skills. For example, some students need additional mini-lessons on sentence structure because when they use their outlines and notes to compose their paragraphs, they just list the details and their sentences tend to run on or to be short and choppy. (For more on revising sentences, see *Language Arts Mini-Lessons*, by Joan Clemmons and Lois Laase; Scholastic, 1995.) Other students need a mini-lesson on how to use transitions to connect the paragraphs and make the writing flow. Additional mini-lessons that need to be revisited by some students include using strong verbs, agreement of subject and verb, writing effective beginning and concluding paragraphs, and organizing the report. When the majority of the class needs one of these lessons, we usually open the writing workshop with it. Otherwise, we provide small-group instruction for students with the same needs.

Saul and Andrew confer about revising the research reports. They help each other clarify some points and point out what they like best.

Working With Peers:
After students have worked alone revising their reports, they must confer with peers. When they're ready for a peer conference, authors write their names on a sign-up sheet. They may work in groups of two or three. In their groups, an author reads her report draft aloud and the partner(s) listens. Often the author will discover something that needs to be fixed while she's reading. Next the listener(s) tells the writer what he liked and what he thinks she did well. He also asks the writer questions to clarify meaning and may offer suggestions. The writer responds and jots notes on her draft for consideration as she continues to revise. Then the authors switch roles. Some students may need a time limit (a fifteen minute period works well) for peer conferences in order to stay on task. As the students confer with peers, they may use a checklist such as the following to help focus the conference on the content of the reports:

Peer Conference Checklist for Reports

Name .... Date ....

Title of Report ....

Partner's Name ....

Questions I asked my partner:	Partner's Responses	
Does my report make sense?	Yes	No
Is it organized in a clear way?	Yes	No
Does it have a good beginning paragraph?	Yes	No
Does all the information belong?	Yes	No
Do you have any questions?	Yes	No
Does my report have a good concluding paragraph?	Yes	No
Did I use interesting, vivid vocabulary?	Yes	No

The Best Research Reports Ever *Scholastic Professional Books, 1998*

Working With the Teacher in Small-Group Writing Conferences: While several peer conferences are occuring in the classroom, we may be meeting with two to four students in a small-group writing conference. These are just like peer conferences except for our presence. As participants in the conference, we listen, offer comments, ask questions, help some students stay focused on the conference, and encourage all group members to participate.

Mrs. Laase participates in a draft revision conference. She listens, comments, and asks questions just as another student would.

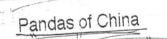

Pandas of China

Did you know that the giant panda belongs to the bear family? Some people think they are a part of the marsupial family, or they are a family of their own, but they aren't. Most people know that all pandas come from China, but from which part? Almost every panda in China comes from Cheng-du which is in the northern part of South China. Some pandas come from North China but not very many. The giant pandas live on the mountains eight thousand feet and when it's winter they move down the mountain to a warmer climate. Only 600 pandas are left in the world.

It takes five months for a giant panda mother to have a baby and when the baby is born they only weigh five to seven ounces and are no bigger then a newborn kitten. A panda only has one panda at a time, and if she has more they are one to two years apart. After the baby is born the mother of the baby will not eat for around twenty-five days. Pandas are seventy pounds at one year and are full grown at three years. A normal size giant panda will weigh about three hundred fifty pounds and are three and one half to five feet tall. Giant pandas are chubby and weigh more then any other mammal it's size. They look like bears but have black and white markings all over their body.

Giant pandas that are wild eat bulbs, roots, eggs, and occasionally small mammals or insects. They also eat twenty pounds of fish and forty pounds of bamboo stalks a day. Every one hundred years bamboo dies and so do most pandas. That is one reason why there are so few pandas left in the World today. Pandas love to eat wild

Lauren has made revisions to the draft of her giant panda report.

We use the anecdotal notes we write during the the small-group conferences later in whole-class meetings to praise students for the parts of their texts they've written especially well and for new techniques they've tried. In addition, small-group conferences give us still another opportunity to notice instructional needs of our students. If we see the same weakness among many students, such as the need to combine ideas in several short sentences into one sentence, we plan a mini-lesson on this for the entire class.

To conclude these mini-lessons, students meet in groups of two to three to revise their drafts, focusing on the skills they've just reviewed. We rotate from group to group giving assistance. Because we established the routine of writing conferences at the beginning of the school year, students feel comfortable conferring with their peers and often informally solicit their advice on a part of the report they're revising.

The Best Research Reports Ever   *Scholastic Professional Books, 1998*

Working With the Teacher Individually: After students have participated in at least one peer conference and revised their drafts following it, we meet individually with each student. At these conferences, which may take place informally at students' desks or as the result of a sign-up sheet, we read their drafts and praise them for writing done well. We ask open-ended questions to get students to reflect, talk, and generate ideas. We also respond to any requests for help as well as

Mrs. Clemmons meets with Laura individually to discuss revising her report. She praises Laura's writing achievements and makes suggestions for improvements.

offer suggestions or review a skill or concept. However, we do not overwhelm students with skills or concepts they need to improve. We focus on just one or two areas, such as adding additional information or revisiting the organization of the report.

Editing the Drafts

When students finish their revisions and are ready to publish or write the final drafts of the reports, we ask them to proofread carefully, checking for information left out, complete sentences, indentation of paragraphs, correct word usage, correct capitalization and punctuation, and correct spelling. We've found that we need to present mini-lessons on some of the following skills to help them edit: sentence fragments, run-on sentences, verb tenses, agreement of subject and verb, use of pronouns, capitalization of proper nouns, correct use of commas, and proper word usage. Depending on who needs them, we conduct these mini-lessons for the entire class, small groups of learners, or individuals. After the authors have edited their own reports, they ask a peer who's good at editing to proofread them. We provide them with the following checklist:

Editing Checklist

___ Are sentences and proper nouns capitalized?   ___ Do the subjects and verbs agree?

___ Are sentences punctuated correctly?   ___ Are all of the words used correctly?

___ Are all of the sentences complete?   ___ Are the words spelled accurately?

___ Are commas used correctly?   ___ Are the paragraphs indented?

The Best Research Reports Ever *Scholastic Professional Books, 1998*

Santos and Jessica edit their reports for publication. They use a dictionary to be sure the words are used correctly and spelled correctly.

We do the final editing in a conference with each student. We ask questions about any errors, for example, "What kind of punctuation mark should you use to separate the items in a list?" We may do a quick mini-lesson or lessons right then on a skill or skills the student still needs. We also note skills the students still need to review.

Publishing the Report

When the editing is completed, students write or type their final drafts, inserting the pictures, charts, and other materials they've selected to enhance their reports. We show them models for listing the various types of resources in their bibliographies. To give the reports a professional polish, they create title pages and include the bibliographies at the end. We encourage students to use the Criteria for Good Report Writing Chart as a final checklist to be sure they've covered all the bases. When final copies are finished, students sit in small groups and proudly share the reports with their classmates.

When Lauren placed her report in her portfolio, she included a self-evaluative statement that reflects her confidence in her ability (see next page).

What can seem to be a steep and difficult mountain to climb becomes only a molehill when students have the necessary instruction, guidance, and support throughout the report-writing process.

Katie and Michelle type their report to get it ready for publication.

80

GIANT PANDAS

Do you know that the giant pandas belong to the bear family?
Some people think they are a part of the marsupial family, but they
aren't. Some scientists place them in the racoon family or in a
family of their own. They can't agree on how to cl___ify them. I
agree with the scientists who say they belong to t___

Most people know that all pandas come from ___
which part? Almost every panda in China comes fr___ Some ___
is in the northern part of South China. The giant pa___
North China but not very many. The giant pa___
mountains eight thousand feet high, and when it's ___
down the mountain to a warmer climate. Unlike no___
don't hibernate in the winter.

It takes five months for a giant panda mot___
When the baby is born in the winter, it only w___
ounces and is no bigger than a newborn kitten. ___
has one panda at a time, and if she has more ___
years apart. After the baby is born, the mot___
not eat for around twenty-five days, because s___
the extra weight.

Pandas are seven pounds at one month and ___
year and are full grown at three years. A no___
will weigh about three hundred fifty pounds ___
half to five feet tall. Giant pandas are ___
than any other mammals their size. They lo___
black and white markings all over their bo___

Pandas sleep twelve to fourteen hour___
almost the whole day. It is also much more ___

Most female pandas are very shy and ee___
funny and out-going and are also very p___
females and males behave differently, the___

When females go into heat, they lea___
rocks. Males also leave scents on trees ___
females. Males also roar loudly to help ___
All giant pandas have bad eyesight.

Giant pandas that are wild eat ___
occasionally small mammals or insects. ___
of fish and forty pounds of bamboo stal___
years bamboo dies and so do most panda___
are so few pandas left in the world too___
mushrooms and sometimes eat mice and ___
pandas eat apples, porridge, carrots, ___
bamboo! Just like wild pandas, they ___

they usually go after the cubs. Fortunately the mothers keep them
in their pouches. Then she climbs a tree to be safe. In other
cases pandas go inside hollow logs to hide and to protect
themselves and their families.

Some pandas given to the U.S.A. are Ling-Ling (female) and
Hsing-Hsing (male). These two lived in the National Zoo. Two
others are Han-Han and Mei-Mei. The first giant panda to come to
the U.S.A. was Su-Lin in the year 1930. When she died, the
zoologists found out that she was a he!

Less than six hundred giant pandas are left in the whole world
today! We need to protect them so we can still go to the zoos and
see them. The wild pandas that are left are happily playing in
South China.

Art (7.___)

Bibliography

Green, Carl. The Giant Panda. Mankato: Crestwood House, 1987.

Grosvenor, Donna. Pandas. Washington: National Geographic, 1973.

"Panda". Microsoft (R) Encarta. Copyright (c) 1994 Microsoft
Corportation. Copyright (c) Funk & Wagnalls Corporation.

Snyder, Gregory. "Pandas". World Book ___ ___ ___icago:
Educational Corporation, 1973.

Evaluation

This piece of writing shows that I can summarize my notes and
write a report. I learned to write an outline and to put what I've
learned into topics. I also know how to revise and edit well and
how to use the thesaurus to help me. I had to fix my verb tenses
many times too! I learned how to scan a picture into my report and
how to write a bibliography. I think I learned a lot about the
giant pandas of China, and I enjoyed it!

Lauren

Lauren's final report on giant pandas illustrates all the skills she learned during the
report-writing process. Her self-evaluation
illustrates the confidence she gained

The Best Research Reports Ever   Scholastic Professional Books, 1998

Providing Ongoing Evaluation

Since evaluation determines the instruction students need to be successful learners, we and our students are continually evaluating throughout the report-writing process.

Teachers: We evaluate students when we observe them at work and when we confer with them. We note their strengths in our anecdotal notes or on a checklist and either address their needs in the conference or plan lessons to help them grow in an identified area.

Students: The students are actively involved in self-evaluation daily when they complete the Self-Evaluation Charts, noting their accomplishments, evaluating their work for the day, making plans for the next day, and requesting help. They do another evaluation at the midpoint of their note-taking to see how they're progressing. When they critically read their reports to revise and edit them and when they participate in peer conferences, they are evaluating their work in order to improve it. After the report is finished, they write a self-evaluative paragraph such as Lauren's (page 81). They are growing as independent learners.

Rubric: A rubric is a rating scale along a continuum for evaluating the quality of work. We and our students develop a rubric for report writing using the Criteria for Good Report Writing to help us. We encourage students to use the rubric to look for ways to improve their reports and, after the final editing is completed, to rate the reports before giving them to us. We use a copy of the same rubric when we make our final evaluation of the report, writing our comments on this rubric rather than on the student papers. The rubric on the following page is the one we and our students developed.

What can be a difficult and steep mountain for some students to climb becomes only a molehill for students who have the necessary instruction, guidance, and support throughout the report-writing process.

The traditional written report is only the beginning. There are myriad ways for different students and different kinds of learners to express the knowledge they've gained from research. Just remember that one of the most important ways to get students motivated to do research is to give them a chance to choose their own topic, whether it's an individual-interest topic or an aspect of a unit with which the class is engaged. The next chapter will describe in detail ten kinds of research projects that our students have enjoyed. Perhaps these will help you devise projects that will enliven and deepen your students' learning.

The Best Research Reports Ever *Scholastic Professional Books, 1998*

Evaluation of My Report

Name .... Date ....

Title of Report ....

Score	Description
5	Beyond expectation—I went way beyond what was expected.
4	Met the expectations—I applied this skill as was expected.
3	Almost there—I had minor problems or omissions.
2	Not quite there—I had major problems or omissions.
1	Not there—I did not complete this part of the assignment.

1 2 3 4 5   I have a good introductory paragraph that meets all the criteria.

1 2 3 4 5   The paragraphs in the body of the report meet all the criteria.

1 2 3 4 5   The paragraphs are arranged in an order that makes sense.

1 2 3 4 5   I have enough information to explain my topic completely.

1 2 3 4 5   The report has a good ending statement in the closing paragraph.

1 2 3 4 5   I used vivid vocabulary.

1 2 3 4 5   My report sounds like me.

1 2 3 4 5   I used pictures, charts, drawings, or diagrams.

1 2 3 4 5   My title page contains the required elements.

1 2 3 4 5   My bibliography is written correctly and is complete.

1 2 3 4 5   The mechanics (capitalization and punctuation) are correct.

1 2 3 4 5   The words are spelled correctly.

1 2 3 4 5   The final copy is typed or written neatly.

The Best Research Reports Ever *Scholastic Professional Books, 1998*

*F*ROM POETRY TO FESTIVALS: 10 GREAT RESEARCH PROJECTS FOR EVERY KIND OF LEARNER

"*I*t was really fun doing research because we got to do projects and fun things to go along with it."

This is what Sarah told us when we asked her about her research experience during the year. Our students enjoy using their research skills to write reports or express themselves in other ways, whether the content is based on a personal interest or is part of a larger project. However, they are particularly excited about working on the large cumulative class projects, such as our Egyptian museum or Greek festival, to which their research contributes and for which they work cooperatively with classmates.

Whatever the project—large or small, about a personal interest or part of a unit, or for a cumulative class project—students may choose to use their research to express themselves in many ways. They may use reports or other written forms—poetry, stories, books, diaries, interviews, descriptions, journals, letters, radio or television scripts, plays, puppet shows, readers' theater, and pantomime. They may construct models, time lines, graphs, and filmstrips, or make costumes for different historical periods.

What's most important is the process that students are learning and their deeper understanding of the information they're studying.

Children frequently choose the visual arts as an expressive form for their knowledge. They may create murals, dioramas, models, illustrations, and cartoons. Others students enjoy giving speeches or oral presentations. Sometimes students incorporate music. Technology, such as the HyperStudio software, enables students to use graphics, text, and sound to produce a program.

The Best Research Reports Ever   *Scholastic Professional Books, 1998*

Ways to Present Research Projects

written report	construct models	readers theater
poetry	time lines	pantomime
stories	graphs	murals
books	scripts for radio and television shows	dioramas
diaries		models
interviews	make costumes for different historical periods	illustrations
descriptions		cartoons
journals	filmstrips	oral presentations
letters	puppet shows	video presentations
plays		

Whatever the format, it isn't the final project that's most important. What's most important is the process that students are learning and using and their deeper understanding of the information they're studying. Authentic research projects encourage students to ponder, review, and concentrate on the information they've learned. Planning and creating the project helps them to clarify their thinking and elaborate on it. It also allows them to use their creative talents.

Students who had researched ancient Greek theater presented a Greek play at our Greek Festival.

Students learn differently and need to express their knowledge in different ways. Sometimes we select the form or forms for a project because we're teaching a specific skill or a particular genre of writing. At other times we encourage our students to select their own method of communicating the information they have learned.

The following examples are just a few of the many research projects we've found to be exciting for our students and valuable teaching tools for us. We hope you can adapt some of the ideas to meet the needs of your students.

Rachel and Kathy explain mummification to guests visiting our ancient Egyptian museum.

The Best Research Reports Ever *Scholastic Professional Books, 1998*

Writing Poetic Responses to Research

Perfection

The Greeks made columns high
Because they worked to perfection
They used a special dye
Because they worked to perfection
The dye was made of spices and milk
Because they worked to perfection
The column's marble felt like silk
Because they worked to perfection.

—Kris

Kris chose to write this poem to share what she had learned from researching Greek architecture. Poetry is one of the favorite forms of writing in our classroom and one of the ways our students choose to share the knowledge they gain from their research. They frequently select poetry because it is an integral part of our classroom.

We begin "teaching" poetry on the first day of school when we read aloud poems related to books and the beginning of school. We continue reading them almost daily and frequently choral read them. Students need to be exposed to poems often. They need to read them and hear them being read. We post poems on charts in our classrooms and make books of poetry available for the students to enjoy reading and sharing.

Students also need to be aware of the beauty and power of words. When we read aloud poetry, we stop, reread passages, and discuss the beauty and the meaning of the language. Then we write some of it on a Vivid Words Chart. After we encourage students to listen for the beautiful and powerful words and phrases, they point them out for inclusion on the chart. We also have a large chart entitled Wonderful Words on which students write vivid verbs, descriptive words, great phrases and similes they find in their readings.

Adam uses his notes to write a poem.

The Best Research Reports Ever *Scholastic Professional Books, 1998*

In mini-lessons, using the overhead projector, we read and study poems and discuss how poets choose words carefully to express ideas and feelings and how a poet seems to paint a picture with words. Some poems make us laugh while others make us sad; some give us information; others tell a story. We enjoy the rhythm and study the comparisons. Some poems rhyme; some don't; others have internal rhyme. We analyze poems to discover the elements of poetry the authors use, and we chart them for reference by category: rhythm, figurative language, imagery, and sound devices such as alliteration and onomatopoeia.

In October on a cool day, we take our writer's notebooks outside to record words and phrases that come to mind as we use our senses to observe our surroundings.

Vivid Words

- sloshing
- fierce
- echoded
- seized
- embrace
- rubbery
- sighing
- grabbing
- jamming
- interlaced
- shrunken
- crawled
- screamed
- scattered
- snapped
- poking
- cinnamon-colored
- nostrils
- widened
- brooding
- growl
- terrified
- slithering
- faint
- brilliant
- wincing

- chalky
- pitiful
- gentlest
- wasteland
- gaping
- like a golden waterfall
- gentle
- quickly
- noble
- intense
- worthy
- thirsty
- glowing
- surprisingly
- roaringly
- leathery
- roughly
- staggering
- ripples
- incredibly
- crest
- roundish
- hunger
- automatically
- persistent

Wonderful Words

Vivid Verbs

- swished
- hustling
- shuffling
- pondered
- bristled
- battered
- revived
- spluttered
- tearing
- flailed
- peering
- whistled
- clasped
- clambered
- beamed
- terrified
- pounding
- thumping
- throbbing
- charging
- contact
- grieving
- beamed
- grabs
- panting
- winced
- pricked
- grabbing
- exploded
- scattered
- crashed
- rustled
- slithering
- scraping
- jerked

Descriptive Words

- omniverous
- turbulent
- hysterically
- vigorously
- immense
- opaque
- melancholy
- opaque
- fearful
- motionless
- thoughtfully
- shrill
- hollow
- motionless
- disobedient
- incapacitated
- lovely
- gloomy
- gigantic
- ruefully
- glistening
- lumpy
- swollen

Great Phrases

- "There is no royal road to geometry."
- In the full flame of autumn's fire
- a battery of sharp white teeth
- never ending music of its bubbling lullaby
- as a puppy on an invisable leash
- glugging river of milk
- with the speed of a salmon
- an ocean of water.
- gurgling song
- A mountain of spotted flesh
- lonely flutey whistles
- straw-colored hair

Similes

- like gigantic stars
- pricked like ice
- he darted off like an arrow
- as fierce as a wolf
- blind as a bat
- Riding the current like a boat
- like a ghost from the mouth of the cave
- air as cold as ice.
- Darted off like an arrow.
- hopped faster than grasshoppers
- As mad as flies in a fruit jar
- Dead as a squashed June bug.
- as rough as worn-out sneakers

The Best Research Reports Ever Scholastic Professional Books, 1998

Change

The wind is whispering,
The leaves are falling,
The air is cool and crisp,
No birds to celebrate the season.

The sky is gray, no kids are playing,
Their toys are left outdoors.
The ground is wet from dew and frost
With rain the sky now pours.

An airplane flies to Florida
Or some other place that's warm,
The birds are now migrating south-
The sense of a snowy storm.

In the distance I hear a dog barking
At the leaves as they fall down.
The leaves are pictured and painted
With orange, yellow, red and brown.

Smoke from the chimneys smells sweet and strong,
The days are short instead of long,
Fall is here, winter, soon.
The seasons singing their changing tune.

The Monument
By Anja

The monument has colorful sides.
Steep cliffs,
Deep canyons
and smooth rocks
make the wind whistle.
Dark shadows
run with the forest green trees.
The blue cloudless sky contrasts
the pointy monoliths
that wrap the monument
like a present at Christmas.
In some spots
the dirt is as red as blood.
The monument is a beautiful place.

No talking is allowed. We look, listen, smell, and sometimes touch the rough tree bark, a smooth slide, or a hairy caterpillar. Inside again we share our observations and write some lovely poetry as Katie did in "Change" and Anja did in "The Monument."

Not only does writing poetry in the content areas integrate the curriculum, but it also reinforces the concepts students learned in their research. They have to understand a topic to be able to write a poem about it. So when they return to their notes for answers to questions, they reinforce their knowledge of the subject. As he composed the quatrains in his poem, "A Tomb Robber," Jimmy demonstrated that he understood the research he'd done.

A Tomb Robber

A Tomb Robber stole jewels from tombs,
The mummy a tomb robber wanted it not.
A tomb robber tore the mummy in bits,
But the jewels; the jewels he wanted a lot.

Tomb Robbing soon became a family crime,
The Robber stole more than a dime,
They stole the jewels to put in their tomb,
To get the jewels they broke into a room.

Punishment for robbing was really severe,
They cut off your hands, your nose, and your ear.
The robber saw what the punishment was,
"Tomb Robbing", "That's all that he does".

The Best Research Reports Ever *Scholastic Professional Books, 1998*

Publishing Alphabet Books

Having students write an alphabet book is a wonderful tool for engaging them in research, and using the format early in the school year is a good way to reinforce organization and paragraph writing skills. There are two effective ways to use this format: (1) Integrate the research for an alphabet book into a unit of study in the content areas. This is a great way to introduce, reinforce and expand vocabulary, as well as reinforce the concepts of the unit. (2) Have students write alphabet books about a topic of special interest to them. Topics that work best have many examples within the category—for example, topics such as snakes, dogs, and airplanes provide children with enough variety to find examples for each letter of the alphabet. In either case, students research their subjects; locate one related word or phrase for each letter of the alphabet; and, finally, create a page for each letter that contains the letter, the word, a paragraph that describes the word, and an illustration. During our science unit, Small Things, students learned to prepare slides of various specimens and use the microscope to observe them. They researched things in the microscopic world, such as algae, bacteria, cells, microbes, and viruses, to include in their alphabet books. Some other alphabet books students have written use vocabulary words from our ancient Egypt and Middle Ages units. Famous people was the topic for an alphabet book by two students working together. Another student made an alphabet book about Colorado.

Before students begin their own alphabet books, we have them read some examples and study the formats. Among a broad collection of alphabet books we gather, we especially like those by Jerry Pallotta. The following books serve as wonderful models: *The Yucky Reptile Alphabet Book* (Charlesbridge, 1989), *The Icky Bug Alphabet Book* (Charlesbridge, 1986), *The Frog Alphabet Book* (Charlesbridge, 1990), and *The Underwater Alphabet Book* (Charlesbridge, 1991). Our students enjoy reading the texts of these books,

Fifth graders are busy at work researching vocabulary to use in their alphabet books.

and they love the beautiful illustrations. As we analyze the formats, we discuss the research the authors had to do to write and illustrate the books. We point out that when Mr. Pallotta visited our school one year, he discussed how he sometimes interviewed specialists such as college professors to gather some of the information. The students decide that because the *Red-eyed*

The Best Research Reports Ever *Scholastic Professional Books, 1998*

Ankh	Ba	Cat	Delta	Egypt	Flail	Gods	Heiroglyf	Isis
• Ankh is symbol of life	• spirt rises from the dead	• cat was very Sacard in Egypt	• Nile Delta goes in Med sea other part in Red Sea	• egypt is in Africa very hot and dry in egypt	• flail is a tool used for threasing wheat and grain	• Egyptians had gods they worshiped	• Heiroglyf were the Egyptians writing language	• the most popular goddes also had ibis head
• Ankh looks like this ↙ [drawing] Ankh	• goes into the after life as a bird	• if you killed a cat you died	• brought water down to River to help people	• very famous for pyramids and mummies	• symbol of office for the pharoah	• many gods the egyptians worshiped	• Over 100 heroglyf used in Egypt	• had a husband Orisis marrie to god of nile
• king tut had mirro shaped like Ankh		• made gods out of cats		• most of egypt has been modernized from acheint times	• used for reap the pertialty	• many had heads of animals		• looke like ibis + thoth

Tree Frog is so unusual this may be one that Mr. Pallotta had to ask an expert about before including it for *R* in his *Frog Alphabet Book* (Charlesbridge, 1990).

> *R is for Red-eyed Tree Frog. This frog might be the most awesome of all the Central and South American rain forest frogs. If people keep cutting down the rain forests, these beautiful frogs will have no place to live.*

When students write an alphabet book as part of a unit of study, we begin early in the unit and integrate the process throughout the study. The students start by writing the alphabet—one letter above each column—across the top of their note-taking grids. They need several sheets taped together for these grids. As students read about their topics and discover words that they'll use to represent

Alex is using his notes to draft paragraphs for his alphabet book.

the letters, they write these words next to their letters. Continuing throughout the unit, students do their research and note the important facts about each word in the appropriate columns on their grids. They'll use these notes to write a good descriptive paragraph for each word. Because they'll be illustrating the terms in their alphabet books, they include sketches on their note-taking grids too.

Before drafting the paragraphs that will be on each page of their alphabet books, students identify who their readers will be. Often they write for younger students. At this point, we reinforce effective paragraph writing with mini-lessons on the skill. Besides using our own notes to demonstrate how to write a descriptive paragraph, we use paragraphs from Jerry Pallotta's books as models.

F is for Fire-bellied Toad. When this toad wants to scare off another animal, it leans its head back and shows its bright red belly. It may look like it has red nail polish on, but frogs do not have fingernails.

> *The Frog Alphabet Book* by Jerry Pallotta
> (Charlesbridge, 1990)

S is for Skink. Everyone has heard of a skunk but how many people have heard of a Skink? On this page is a Blue-tongued Skink. It did not get its blue tongue from licking blue lollipops. It was born this way.

> *The Yucky Reptile Book* by Jerry Pallotta
> (Charlesbridge, 1989)

After their drafts are completed, the students, meeting in small conference groups, revise and edit their descriptive paragraphs. When they're satisfied with their work, they begin publishing. When a student completes his published pages, they are bound on a bookbinding machine or with yarn or rings into a book that he proudly shares with other students.

Besides providing research practice, writing an alphabet book is particularly helpful in giving students meaningful opportunities to use the vocabulary. Instead of relying on dictionary definitions, which usually lack enough

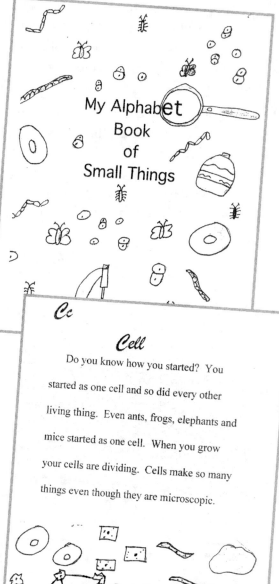

91

information to make the concepts understandable, students are engaged in an in-depth process that actively involves them in learning meanings of new words. When they thoroughly understand the meanings of new words, students' reading comprehension is enhanced.

• • • • • • • • •

Interviewing Historical Figures

When students research historical figures, they enjoy presenting what they learn as an interview on a TV news program. The researcher plays the historical figure, dressed in the style of his or her time period. Classmates play the role of the newscasters conducting the interview. The interviews are videotaped for review and evaluation and for the fun of seeing the performances again.

We study ancient Greece, so our students choose a great Greek to research. Because many of the famous Greeks were mathematicians and scientists, we're able to integrate our math and science curriculums with social studies and language arts for many aspects of this project. We require students to include in their presentations the reason the person became famous, and how our lives have been influenced by what he did. They may also include anything else they think will make the interview more interesting.

Adam wrote his notes about Hippocrates on a note-taking grid.

The Best Research Reports Ever Scholastic Professional Books, 1998

When students have finished taking their notes, they organize them by topic and use them to prepare questions covering what they've learned. Some students choose to write answers to the questions as scripts that they can refer to during the interviews. Others simply refer directly to their notes, which they organize in the same order the questions will be asked. We encourage students to study the information so well that they'll only need to refer to their notes occasionally. Adam researched Hippocrates and, using his notes, wrote the following questions.

Jonathan prepares a prop to use in the interview.

1. When and where were you born?
2. How did you become a doctor?
3. What is the Hippocratic Oath?
4. If your patient was ill, what did you tell him to do to cure himself?
5. What kind of tools did you use when you operated?
6. How were your ideas different from other doctors of your time?
7. How have our lives today in the 20th century been influenced by what you did?

After they have their questions or scripts, the students practice the interviews with partners until they feel comfortable. Each partner gets to be a newscaster as well as a great Greek.

Additional preparations include fashioning costumes that reflect the historical period and training student volunteers to use the video camera. Some students place props such as inoperable microphones on the table as part of the set. Others prepare transparencies for the overhead projector to help explain concepts. For example, "Pythagoras" prepared a transparency to help explain his theorem. When they are ready, students write their names and the dates and times of their interviews on a sign-up sheet.

Tyler interviews "Homer" on the Greek News program.

Samantha dresses as Pythagoras and uses a transparency to explain his theorem.

The Best Research Reports Ever *Scholastic Professional Books, 1998*

Camera girl, Sara, videotapes a historical interview.

With the camera on the tripod, the cameraman (student videotaper) signals action, and the interviews begin with the newscaster's welcome to *Greek News*. We prompt the classmates to watch carefully and write notes about the important accomplishments of each great Greek and how our lives have been influenced by him. They use their notes to write responses in their learning logs. Eunji concluded her notes with, "The interviews were fun. I'll never forget these great Greeks."

After enjoying watching themselves on the video, our students self-evaluate their interviews. We also have a checkout system for taking the video home to share with parents. TV interviews are not only a fun way to share knowledge, but they also sharpen learners' interviewing and public speaking skills.

Creating a Question-and-Answer Book

We publish a question-and-answer big book as a culminating activity for our science study of dinosaurs and their characteristics. However, this is a wonderful way for students to use their research skills to internalize the content of any unit.

Sometimes we introduce our students to the project by showing them a question-and-answer big book borrowed from a primary classroom. Other times we discuss the game *Jeopardy*, for which contestants have to think of a question that answers a specific clue. Students

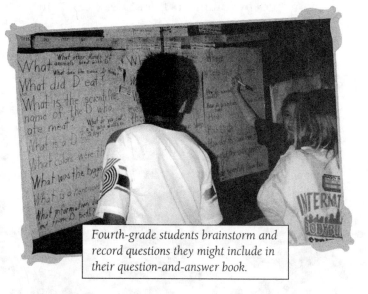

Fourth-grade students brainstorm and record questions they might include in their question-and-answer book.

pattern our class book along the lines of *Jeopardy*. They formulate questions that can be answered with facts they've learned in their science unit.

To help students understand the concept of the question-and-answer book, we model the first one or two questions. Then we have a brainstorming session to come up with questions for the

The Best Research Reports Ever *Scholastic Professional Books, 1998*

Evan and his partner finalize their question-and-answer page.

Alonso and Hillary search through books to find information to answer their question.

book. Students look at their science folders, where they keep materials and any notes they may have taken during the study of dinosaurs, and at the science material around the room to reflect on everything they've studied about dinosaur characteristics. As students verbalize questions, we record them on chart paper. Here are some typical questions from our students:

How do paleontologists know if dinosaurs lived in herds or by themselves?

How can the position of the eyes tell whether a dinosaur ate meat or grass?

What effect does the tail have on the way a dinosaur walked?

Who found the first dinosaur bone?

How can paleontologists tell how large a dinosaur was?

The students decided that a plain, simple cover would be best for their book.

How color protected the dinosaur is the topic for Jon's page of the big book.

95

After the questions are determined, each student chooses one to answer. Most of the information in their answers comes from the knowledge they've gained during our study of dinosaurs; however, we require them to have at least two references so the answers will include plenty of details.

After going through the researching, drafting, conferring, revising, and editing steps, each student or group of students prepares his answer for the big book. The students use a computer to write the final copy, making each page similar by using the same font and font size. A large font is used for the question and a smaller font for the answer. On another sheet of paper, a colorful illustration is made. Each group is then responsible for laying out their page, using glue to position the question, answer, and illustration. We use 12" x 18" sheets of construction paper for our pages. Students volunteer to make a cover and the table of contents. The book is then bound by using a bookbinding machine, inserting rings, or tying with yarn.

In a culminating review of the unit, each student shares his question-and-answer page with his peers and answers any additional questions they have about the topic. Writing a big book and sharing the material is a wonderful way for students to internalize the information from a specific unit of study. It also gives students experience in using another expository writing style. Students take turns taking the book home to share with family members. A note on the outside encourages parents to write their comments.

Producing a Filmstrip Complete with Sound

Making a class filmstrip is a creative way for students to assemble data from a unit of study. They combine their speaking, writing, and artistic skills to produce an audio visual they can share with others. We produce our filmstrip after we've immersed ourselves in the study of the Anasazi culture.

We begin by thinking about the information we have learned about the culture and then brainstorm for topics we might consider including in our filmstrip. Soon our chalkboard is filled with words like kiva, pottery, education, clothing, sipapu, food, weapons, climate, housing, and petroglyphs.

The next step is the planning stage. How are we going to present these topics on a filmstrip? Realizing that writing information on a filmstrip is difficult, the students decide to record their written reports on an audiotape and draw related pictures on the film. Then each student selects a topic that interests him and begins the process of researching in depth.

After the researching, drafting, and editing processes are complete, the students begin to work on the actual filmstrip. First they make a pattern by drawing pictures that illustrate their topics

on plain white paper. Next, each student places his pattern under a clear transparency (the kind used on an overhead projector) and uses permanent, fine-tipped overhead markers to trace and color their pictures. The transparencies are then taped together. The students record their written narrative on an audio tape, making certain that the audio parts are recorded in the same order as the pictures. As they record, they ring a soft bell at the end of each oral presentation to indicate that the filmstrip should be moved ahead. We project the finished filmstrip on the screen of the overhead projector while the tape recorder plays the sound. Parents make a great audience, so we always share our filmstrip at our student-led conferences. Other classes enjoy the filmstrip, too.

Jimmer and Jay, two fourth graders, use a Colorado textbook to research their topic.

Here's the report that Brit recorded:

> The Anasazi wore very few clothes. The women wore small string aprons in the warmer months, while the men wore loin cloths. Large blankets were woven from thin strips of fur to be used with animal skin robes during the colder weather. The children wore nothing in the summer but they did wear clothing in the winter. They wore jewelry made from stones, turquoise, seashells, bones, and seeds.

Making an audio filmstrip is a wonderful way for students to express their knowledge. It also taps into students' speaking and creative art skills.

• • • • • • • • • • •

Turning Fact into Historical Fiction

Estella wants to know if she can use the book *What's the Big Idea Ben Franklin?*, a historical fiction book written by Jean Fritz (Scholastic, 1976), as a reference for research she's doing on Ben Franklin for her science class. There couldn't be a better time for teaching the difference between fact and historical fiction and to introduce the idea of using research to create a historical fiction book or story.

97

First, we teach students what historical fiction is and how to distinguish fact from fiction. Using the historical fiction book we're reading aloud about Hahnee, an Anasazi boy, students begin recording all the historical facts they recognize in the story. They make another list for the parts they know are not historical facts—in other words, those that are fictitious. The lists look like this:

Hahnee—fiction	Hahnee—fact
—no real Hahnee	—hunted small game with bow and arrow
—no dog named Mozo	—water jugs to catch rain in
—probably no word like funny head	—wise elders
—map	—used snares
—red bag	—kivas

The lists continue to grow as we read through the book. The students are impressed with all the facts they learn about the Anasazi culture as they enjoy listening to a good story about Hahnee. To further clarify the distinctions between historical fiction and nonfiction, we make a Venn diagram comparing and contrasting the two genres. We post the Venn diagram and the lists as references.

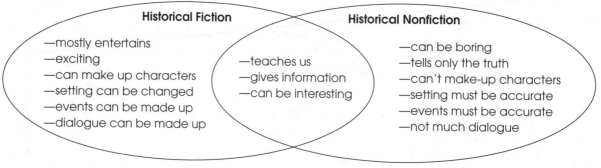

Historical Fiction
—mostly entertains
—exciting
—can make up characters
—setting can be changed
—events can be made up
—dialogue can be made up

—teaches us
—gives information
—can be interesting

Historical Nonfiction
—can be boring
—tells only the truth
—can't make-up characters
—setting must be accurate
—events must be accurate
—not much dialogue

The students are excited when they hear they'll have an opportunity to write their own historical fiction. We begin by using the Venn diagram to discuss styles for writing a factual piece. We read paragraphs from an encyclopedia, a textbook, and a nonfiction trade book. If possible, we use books that relate to the topic of study. Next, we write a group paragraph. Let's say we're writing about clay pottery, which is part of our study of the Anasazi culture. As we write our paragraph, we make certain that we include information about where the pots have been found and about their color, design, shape, use, and so on. After we've agreed on a factual paragraph, students volunteer to make up and tell a story about the clay pots, remembering that fictional stories have characters, settings, conflicts, and resolutions. It's exciting to hear the stories grow and develop as students piggyback on their classmates' ideas.

When everyone feels comfortable with the assignment of writing their own piece of historical fiction, each student chooses a topic of inquiry. Students choose their topics in various ways. Some look at our list of Anasazi words; others look through the material available in the room; still others brainstorm with a friend or ask for teacher assistance.

To begin, students use a note-taking grid to research and record facts about their topic and then draft an expository paragraph or paragraphs. After revising and editing these paragraphs, they begin the second part of the assignment—using their facts to write historical fiction. Again, students draft, revise, and edit. Before they publish both the factual and fictional papers, the authors share their pieces with a partner or a small group. Hearing themselves read a manuscript aloud and considering the listeners' questions and suggestions helps the authors improve their papers to meet the Criteria for Good Report Writing (see page 72).

After the expository and fictional writings are published, students share them with a partner. The partner reads the expository text; then, the author reads the fictional part, adding voice inflections as desired.

Jan wrote the following expository paragraph about a kiva and then turned the facts into a delightful fictional story entitled "The Spirits Will Get You."

KIVA

An Anasazi village has an underground room that is only for men and older boys. No women or girls are allowed in the room. This room is called a kiva. There is a hole in the ground where they can enter the kiva. A ladder is used to climb down into the room.

The room is used for religious ceremonies. There is a hole in the floor called a sipapu. The Anasazi believe the spirits enter and leave from the sipapu. The men and boys use the kiva for gambling.

THE SPIRITS WILL GET YOU

"You can't go into the kiva," said Hahnoo to his sister, Sanee, as he was about to lower himself down a ladder into the kiva.

"What do you do down in the kiva?" asked Sanee.

"You are a girl and it is only for older boys and men."

"Oh please," begged Sanee, "tell me what it is used for."

"Oh fine, since you are begging, I'll tell you," he whispered. "We have religious ceremonies. We believe in the spirits. There is a small hole in the ground called a sipapu where the spirits can come and go."

"Do you do anything else down there?" asked Sanee.

"Yes, we gamble too, but I have to go now and trade for a new atlatl." So Hahnoo left the kiva and met his friends to trade.

After he walked off a spirit rose out of the sipapu and said, "It's O.K., Sanee. Come down here and see the kiva for yourself but don't tell anybody or you will have to go to the council." So Sanee went down the ladder and saw everything.

When students create both expository and fictional pieces and see them side by side, they have a very clear feeling for the distinction between fact and fiction. Besides using their research skills in an exciting way, they learn to read historical fiction with new understanding.

Creating Biographical Sketches Brought to Life Through Half-Size Portraits

For this research project, students become a famous person in history through their self-drawn portraits and biographical sketches. The project combines the Half-Size Me Portrait activity (a Marilyn Burns math exercise that teaches drawing to scale) with art and research to create an authentic research project. We use the results to decorate the hallways for our grade-level program for parents.

We begin the project by brainstorming a list of famous people students have read or heard about during their study of Colorado history. Some students look through tables of contents and indexes in reference books to find names the rest of us haven't thought of. Kit Carson, Escalante and Charles Bent are just a few of the names that appear on the list.

After each student has chosen a person to "bring to life," we review the research process. Students follow the same research, drafting, revising, and editing formats they use for research papers or other projects.

As the students are researching, they learn how to use the Half-Size Me Portrait activity to draw a figure that is exactly half the size of themselves. Each student needs a large sheet of paper (36" x 24"), a piece of string about 20 inches long, and a partner. The students begin by using their string to measure the length of their partner's face. That length, folded in half, will be the length of the face

Megan poses in front of her portrait of Chipeta, an Indian famous in Colorado history. Megan did a lot of reading about Chipeta. Through her research, she knew how to design Chipeta's costume and discovered interesting facts to include in the biographical sketch.

Molly Brown, a famous lady in Colorado history, is the topic of this Half-Size Me project.

After completing his research, Chris knew how to design the clothes for his mountain man.

on the paper. Then students measure the width of the face, eyes, nose, mouth, ears, arms, wrists, fingers, shoulders, legs, and so on and halve these measurements to determine their sizes for the portrait. The artists grow more and more excited as they see a miniature of themselves appear on their papers.

Designing an authentic costume for the famous person is the next step. A question on everyone's note-taking grid is "What type of clothing did my famous person wear?" Soon the figures are outfitted in buckskin, long flowing skirts, mountain man attire, and so on. Crayons or pastel chalks work best for adding color. Since the background is usually messy, students cut out the completed portraits and mount them on colorful pieces of fadeless paper. Students then glue their published biographical sketches next to the portraits. The finished products, which required a combination of social studies, language arts, math, and art skills, are displayed with pride in the school hallways.

* * * * * * * * * *

Publishing Brochures

Sandy Cruz, a resource teacher, uses a computer program to design brochures that students use their research skills to write. The brochures, which are written for kids and describe students' communities, are so professional that real estate companies are now including them in their packets for newcomers, and the local visitors' bureau is handing them out to tourists.

Through group discussions, students share what they already know about their city or locality. Since there isn't any information about Grand Junction in text books, the teachers and students

The Best Research Reports Ever *Scholastic Professional Books, 1998*

gather reference material in the form of pamphlets, brochures, and promotional material. The local Chamber of Commerce is a great source for acquiring this material. Students also look at the Grand Junction Web page for additional information. The teachers choose sections of this material to read to the class, which stimulates discussions and develops students' background knowledge. City officials are also invited to visit the classroom to share their expertise.

Most of this unit of study is conducted in the classroom, but Sandy arranges for the students to visit

Resource teacher Sandy Cruz shares information about Grand Junction with the class.

five localities of their choice for more in-depth research. The students decide where to visit by brainstorming answers to this question: "What do you find fascinating about our city, and what parts of the city would you like to know more about?" When the list is narrowed to five places, the teachers ask the students if they'd like to make a brochure using the information they obtain from these visits. Because students are intrigued now and have had a part in making the choices, their interest is high. They're eager to begin.

Dinosaur Valley

362 Main
241-9210

Grand Junction is a great place to learn about dinosaurs. They used to live around here you know. One great place to visit is Dinosaur Valley. You can dig up your own fossils and see how really humongous they were. One dinosaur talks -- he'll tell you how fast he is. You see all kinds of rocks and minerals that are found in this area. You may be really surprised! You

Columbine Students having fun at Dinosaur Valley

can watch paleontologists at work! Don't forget to stop at the Gift Shop. There are lots of cool dinosaur stuff to buy.

Museum of Western Colorado

4th and Ute • 242-0971

The museum "tells" the story of Grand Junction as you walk around and see the displays. You can learn about the Native Americans that once lived in this valley. Learning about the settlers that followed the Native Americans and how they made Grand Junction into a town is interesting.

Going to school a hundred years ago at the museum

You can learn about the famous people that helped put Grand Junction on the map. If you choose to live in Grand Junction, it won't take long until you find out about the peaches and other delicious fruit that are grown in this valley. You can learn how that industry got started in our area. It is fun to look at all the old pictures and see how people and buildings have changed over time. The museum is a great place to go. It will give you an understanding of how Grand Junction came to be.

Production compliments of the UTP Graphics Communications Department

Here is what students from Columbine Elementary think is important for KIDS to know...

Grand Junction Is A FUN PLACE for KIDS!

This brochure was written by students in Geri Lovelace's class.

Since it's not feasible to take the whole class to all five sites, the teachers make the necessary business contacts and arrange to accompany small groups to each site. The group for each site is then responsible for reporting back to the rest of the class. In advance, the students prepare a list of questions they want answered and things they want to see. For example,

here are some of the questions the students wanted to ask the people who ran Laser Storm, an amusement center:

- Is there an admission fee?
- Is age an admission requirement at Laser Storm?
- How are the games played?
- Where do you get the games?
- Are any of the games dangerous?

At a site, each member of the group is responsible for asking one or two questions and taking notes. Students also take

These boys pay a visit to the City Parks office, where they receive information about the Grand Junction parks.

photographs. Back at school, each student drafts the answer to his or her question, keeping in mind that the brochure is directed to other kids. The next day, the students share their written research with other members of their group, and together, they combine the information into one or more well-written paragraphs. The teachers give students a review mini-lesson on writing an introductory sentence that will grab the readers' attention and make them want to continue reading. After they write their initial drafts, the students confer, revise, and edit. They work until they have a polished piece ready for inclusion in the brochure.

There are computer programs that the students use to lay out their own brochures. However, Sandy doesn't have the equipment in school to scan pictures and do the actual printing, so she arranges with students at the local vocational education program to help with the finished product. After Sandy's students input the material on the classroom computer, a small group, the publishing committee, takes their disks and pictures to the students at the local vocational education center. Together, both groups scan pictures, determine the font, lay out the entire brochure, and design the cover. The cost of the printing is covered by a donation.

Computer Tip
When several students need to add information to the same document, it's faster if each of them writes and saves it on his own disk. That way, several students can key in their information at the same time using different computers. Then it's a simple process to use the computer's copy-and-paste program to transfer all the pieces to one document. Once all the information is on one disk, it's easy to determine the font and font size and to work on a layout design.

The Best Research Reports Ever *Scholastic Professional Books, 1998*

The brochure project involves students in authentic research and writing. As they write, they are organizing and clarifying their thoughts. They have a purpose for their visits to different areas of the city, and they use the information they learn in a meaningful way.

• • • • • • • • •

Using the Internet and Local Mentors as a Catalyst for Individual Research

Sandy Cruz, in her role as a resource teacher, works with students in different classrooms, challenging them to work to their full potential. The individual research project described here could be used by students of different abilities and interests and by the whole classroom or individual learners working on their own.

To begin, Sandy meets with individual students or with groups of two or three and asks what interests them most and least. Through a conversation with Sandy, Kristen pinpoints her favorite subjects—art, math, and science, especially the study of space. Emily, an outdoor person, is especially interested in ranching. Jake likes snakes, and Timmy's interests are similar to Kristen's. Based on these interests, the students each determined a topic for research and planned a project that would illustrate their research discoveries. With individual research projects such as these, it's important that students have a keen interest in their topics because they'll be working on their own or with a mentor most of the time. The projects described here are those that Timmy, Kristen, Emily, and Jake did to supplement their classroom curriculum. Sandy Cruz gave support and guidance as needed.

Kristen's and Timmy's Cities: After doing some background reading and talking with Sandy, their peers, and their parents, Kristen and Timmy both decide to design and build unique cities, addressing their concern that the world is becoming overpopulated. "There are just too many people," Kristen lamented. So she decided to put her city in space. For the same reason, Timmy decided to build his city underwater. In addition to resource material in the library, the Internet and members of the community become resources for both of these students. Since both Kristen and Timmy decided on similar research topics, they were able to work together and share many of their resources. They began by researching what other countries are doing about overpopulation. They visited with a local city planner and other city officials to hear what was happening in their own backyard. They asked questions about sewers and electricity. They wanted to know how much space is required for each person to live and how much agricultural space is needed to feed these people. Other questions Kristen and Timmy asked included: "What kind of transportation system is needed to get people to the city in space or underwater?" "What kind of security system does the city need?" and "What psychological effects will living in an enclosed city have on the inhabitants?" The more research they did,

the more questions they had. By the end of the project, their note-taking grids were huge, with several pieces of paper taped together to hold all of their notes.

The Internet proved to be the best source for both Timmy and Kristen. It takes some scouting by the teacher to locate Internet mentors, but they are out there. Through a conference she attended, Sandy located a NASA scientist to serve as Kristen's mentor and through

Emily and Kristen check a reference for information

her university contacts she found a professor at the University of Texas to mentor Timmy. E-mail dialogues went back and forth between mentors and students. For example, Kristen worried about how the people in her space city would be able to move around without gravity. The NASA scientist suggested that if she would spin her city, it would create its own gravity. Kristen worried that the spinning would make people dizzy and contacted her mentor to discuss her concerns.

After researching for most of a semester, Kristen and Timmy were ready to write about their discoveries and to build their cities. Using their note-taking grids and going through the writing process, they condensed their information into well-written reports. Reflecting on their research information, Timmy and Kristen were able to build replicas of their cities as they envisioned them. Timmy plastered and painted the inside of a box to simulate an underwater setting. He even designed an underground escape system. Although he only built one house in his city, it was an example of how he perceived a house might look in an under-

Timmy shares information about his underwater city with a younger student.

The Best Research Reports Ever   *Scholastic Professional Books, 1998*

water situation. Kristin used blocks and pegs to build a layered city for outer space. She found a craftsman who built a Plexiglass dome to go around her city so it could spin in space.

They invited the city officials they'd interviewed to school to see the finished products and to hear about the research that went into the building of the cities. Kristen and Timmy had a genuine audience that was truly interested in their research.

Emily's Sheep Ranch: Because of her love of ranching, Emily decided to develop a sheep ranch. Sandy located a mentor for her, a faculty member of the local college with a background in agricultural livestock. The two conversed by phone and visited with each other. Emily's mother helped by driving Emily to visit her mentor. Sometimes the two visited places where sheep were being raised. Emily researched her two main concerns: Where should she locate her ranch? What kinds of sheep would be the best for the ranch? Through a study of different geographical areas, she determined that Ohio would be the best place for her sheep ranch. Emily's final presentation included a written report that justified her reasons for choosing Ohio and described the type of sheep she would breed to suit the conditions in Ohio. As a visual, she prepared a board with pictures and descriptions of the different types of sheep.

Jake's Snake Project: Some students who think they want to undertake individualized research are not yet ready for so much independent work. Jake was just such a student. He started out with great enthusiasm and drive to research snakes and build a zoo to house snakes for his project. But he didn't follow through. Sandy realized that Jake needed more structure and teacher guidance than a mentor can provide. He was guided to do a more structured research project.

Mentors, whether they're from the local community or are Internet sources, can be valuable resources for the students as they do research—especially individualized research. Mentors provide students with places to go to find answers to their questions, and they provide an interested audience for students' final projects. A word of caution, however: All mentors, especially E-mail mentors, should be screened by teachers and parents.

Timmy, Kristen, and Emily check out an E-mail message.

The Best Research Reports Ever *Scholastic Professional Books, 1998*

Web Sites for Primary Sources

The National Archives and Records Administration encourages educators to visit our Web site at http://www.nara.gov

....

The following Web sites contain additional information about primary sources and links to digitized images and documents:

The Presidential Libraries
http://www.nara.gov/nara/president/address.html

Project Whistlestop (Harry S. Truman Library)
http://www.whistlestop.org

National History Day
http://www.thehistorynet.com/NationalHistoryDay/

The Library of Congress
http://www.loc.gov/

Thomas: Legislative Information on the Internet
http://thomas.loc.gov/

The White House
http://www.whitehouse.gov/WH/Welcome.html

Repositories of Primary Sources
http://www.uidaho.edu/special-collections/Other.Repositories.html

Ready, Net, Go! Internet Resources for Archives
http://www.tulane.edu/~1miller/ArchivesResources.html

Archives and Archivists
http://www.muchio.edu/archiveslist/

World Wide Web Virtual Library—History
http://history.cc.ukans.edu/history/WWW_history_main.html

History Computerization Project
http://www.directnet.com/history/

The Gallery of the Open Frontier: Digital Graphics and Photographs of the American West, 1861-1912, from the collections of the National Archives
http://www.uni.edu/UP/gof/unp-aw.htm

Maryland State Archives
http://www.mdarchives.state.md.us/

The Best Research Reports Ever *Scholastic Professional Books, 1998*

A Few Good Web Sites

Teachers have used the following Web sites with success. Many of the history sites include primary sources such as documents, diaries, and maps.

HISTORY
American Revolution to Reconstruction
http://grid.let.rug.nl/~welling/usa/revolution.html

Archiving Early America
http://earlyamerica.com/

American Civil War Home Page
http://funnelweb.utcc.utk.edu/~hoemann/cwarhp.html

Welcome to the Civil War Center
http://www.cwc.lsu.edu/

Suffrage History
http://www.pbs.org:80/onewoman/suffrage.html

Women in World History Curriculum by Lyn Reese
http://home.earthlink.net~womenwhist/index.html

GEOGRAPHY
Map Quest
http://www.mapquest.com/

The Teaching Learning Web (U.S. Geological Service)
http://www.usgs.gov/education/learnweb/index.html

...AND ACROSS THE CURRICULUM
The Invention Dimension
http://web.mit.edu/invent/

National Flags
http://155.187.10.12/flags/nation-flags.html

Making Research Come Alive with Museums and Festivals

Beginning on the day we introduce our unit on ancient Egypt and decide to develop a museum as the culminating activity, students begin preparing with great anticipation. They're excited about becoming experts on topics of their choice. They're enthusiastic about working with classmates interested in the same general topic to create a project for the museum. They know that the museum will be open to other students and to parents and that they will serve as docents and use their projects to explain what they learned about their topics.

After being immersed in the unit for several days, students have many questions and have identified lots of topics they can hardly wait to investigate. They wonder: Why did the Egyptians make mummies and how were they made? Why did they build pyramids? How did

The Best Research Reports Ever *Scholastic Professional Books, 1998*

they build them? What did they eat? What was their life like? What did they do for recreation? These questions and others are the catalyst for developing the museum.

Now each student chooses a general area to research, and based on these choices, the students form small groups of two to four. For example, students interested in exploring questions about everyday life are grouped together. If more than four students choose the same

Rachel and Jennifer created authentic masks and costumes to wear as they explained their research topic, theater in ancient Greece.

area, more groups are formed. After explaining what he already knows about the area, each group member identifies a specific question or topic he wants to research. For example, the students in the everyday life group had these questions: What were the Egyptians' homes like? What kind of clothes did they wear? How were the children educated? What did they do for recreation?

Next, each student brainstorms a list of questions related to her specific topic. For example, Samantha had these questions about her topic, recreation in ancient Egypt: What sports did they play? What kind of clothes and equipment did they have for the sports? What did they do in their spare time?

Each learner puts his questions above the squares on his note-taking grid, and the research process begins. The group members are very supportive of one another as they share materials and any information they find that relates to another member's topic.

When students finish gathering their information, each group member teaches the others in his group what he learned. With note-taking grids in hand, the group discusses and decides on an

Ayesha and Michelle assist each other with research.

Lauren and Eun-Ji create their project.

Jonathan and Kevin discuss possible projects they can create that will assist them in explaining their research.

appropriate project they can make for the museum. Models of homes, pyramids, and mummies, as well as food, costumes, masks, and headpieces, are some of the projects chosen. They discuss the various jobs necessary for completing the project and agree on the duties of each member. Each group also writes a letter at this time inviting parents and other students to visit the museum.

Striving to complete the projects on time, students work cooperatively in the classroom, hallway, or any spot they can find. They decide on Egyptian costumes to wear, and some students make parts of the costumes at school. Parent volunteers make it possible to work outside the classroom in such areas as hallways and resource rooms.

Before the museum opens, the group members use their note-taking grids to formulate statements or questions to guide their presentations. These will be posted to give the guests ideas about what to discuss or ask. The jewelry and clothing group made the following chart:

Heather, Eun-Ji, and Michelle shared tidbits of Egyptian food with guests in the "museum."

The Best Research Reports Ever *Scholastic Professional Books, 1998*

Jewelry and Clothing

ASK US ABOUT...

- what men liked to wear.
- why they wore jewelry.
- how they made jewelry.
- what clothes the pharaohs wore.
- what the clothes were made out of.
- what jewelry the pharaohs wore.
- what they wore on special occasions.

A couple of days before the grand opening, students bring in cloths to cover their desks, which have been pushed together to make tables for displays. They put finishing touches on scrolls they've written in hieroglyphics to identify their topics. The groups, some in costumes, practice their presentations by giving them to the rest of the class. The classmates write notes as they listen, and they may ask the experts questions at the conclusion of each presentation. To reinforce the concepts they learn from each other, we have students explain the important ideas they heard in learning log entries.

Finally, the day we have been anticipating arrives. The classroom looks like a real museum. Students have covered the bulletin boards with murals that depict the Egyptian style of art and made the classroom door look like the entrance to a pyramid. The displays on the cloth-covered tables include the students' projects and some nonfiction

Rachel, Kathy, and Danny discuss mummification in ancient Egypt with museum guests.

Lauren, Sarah, and Kimberly discuss art in ancient Egypt with parents visiting the museum.

books they used for research. Proud parents arrive at their appointed time, and the "Egyptian docents" explain their artifacts and the history connected with the displays. When the parents leave, the invited classes begin to arrive.

At the end of a wonderful, exciting day the students talk about how thrilled they are with the museum and all the preparation for it. They enthusiastically ask when they can start their next research project and if they can please have another museum. How wonderful it is to see every student excited about learning!

Kevin, Jonathan, Samantha, and Andrew present a play at our Greek festival.

We agree to culminate the next unit with a similar activity, a Greek Festival. With this project, in addition to presenting the research information, students entertained the guests with plays, some of which were written by students who researched ancient Greek theater. We also enjoyed sampling delicious morsels prepared by the experts on ancient Greek food.

Marissa and Kathy explain the ancient Olympics to parents and visitors at the Greek Festival.

Research projects that end with culminating presentations give students a real sense of accomplishment, and they enable parents to see all the skills their children have developed. Making sure our students have a grasp of the purpose of their research skills and how well they're using these skills is an integral part of our evaluation procedure, which is the subject of our next chapter.

DEVELOPING AND MAINTAINING ASSESSMENTS THAT ARE VALID AND LINKED TO CLASS INSTRUCTION

What teacher doesn't struggle with assessment and evaluation? We certainly do. So we're constantly looking for ways to assess and evaluate student growth.

In the realm of research, we base our evaluation program on the belief that it is important for students to become proficient in researching for and processing information, using this information to write expository material effectively, and using oral language to present factual material in a well-organized and interesting manner. We value the final product, whether it is a list on the board, a short oral presentation, a poem, an interview, or a more in-depth report; however,

Anecdotal notes have no value unless you use them to evaluate accomplishments and needs and plan your lessons accordingly.

we believe that what happens during the process of learning is more important than the finished product. Consequently, we've developed tools to chart our students' progress throughout the process. Sometimes we use just one assessment; other times, we use a combination of several tools. As we assess the data, we're able to evaluate our students' progress and guide their learning. Here are the assessments we use.

The Best Research Reports Ever   *Scholastic Professional Books, 1998*

Anecdotal Notes

After experimenting with several methods for keeping anecdotal records, we found one that works best for us. We divide a sheet of paper into sections and put a student's name in each section. We list the names alphabetically by first names. This serves as our master copy, and we use a new sheet each time we observe our students in a meaningful learning experience. As we look over the students' note-taking grids, we record comments such as "able to pick out main ideas," "needs additional help to locate important points," or "reading comprehension seems to be a stumbling block." When conferring with students on their drafts, we make comments on mechanics, flow, descriptive words, and so on. A note might read "confused on keeping like facts in one paragraph." Anecdotal notes are also a good way to record what you hear and observe during an oral presentation. But like all assessment tools, anecdotal notes have no value unless you use them to evaluate accomplishments and needs and plan your lessons accordingly.

Checklists

To be effective, checklists have to be student generated. For example, when we work with students on writing effective paragraphs, we and the students develop a chart, similar to the one below, that lists all the elements an effective paragraph should include:

Editing My Paragraph

My paragraph

—has one topic.	Yes	No
—has a topic sentence.	Yes	No
—has supporting sentences that give details or facts about the topic.	Yes	No
—has vivid words.	Yes	No
—has complete sentences.	Yes	No
—has sentences that make sense and stick to the topic.	Yes	No
—has sentences that are in an order that makes sense.	Yes	No
—is made up of sentences that flow.	Yes	No
—has the words spelled correctly.	Yes	No
—has correct punctuation.	Yes	No
—has correct capitalization.	Yes	No
—is indented.	Yes	No

The Best Research Reports Ever *Scholastic Professional Books, 1998*

Students use this checklist to help them determine whether all the elements are present and to remind them to include any that are absent. We use the same checklist to assess whether the student shows mastery in writing paragraphs or to determine areas we can help with.

These checklists can be reproduced so that students can check off each element, or they can be put on charts for the students to refer to as they assess their work. Checklists tell whether an element is there or not. They don't evaluate in the qualitative sense. They just say "yes" the element is present or "no" it's not. When our students and their editing partners are assessing the six traits of writing, they use the Editing Checklist on the following page.

Checklists don't evaluate in the qualitative sense. They just say "yes" the element is present or "no" it's not.

Rubrics

A rubric is a rating scale along a continuum for evaluating quality of work. Rubrics make expectations explicit because they measure established guidelines for performance. Rubrics are especially helpful when we're assessing finished projects or oral presentations, because they help us focus on the process and not just the product. We work with students to create appropriate rubrics early in the process of starting a unit or project so that students, teachers, and parents know the requirements and expectations for the projects.

Our rating scale is based on a scale of one to five. A five indicates that the student went beyond expectations. We like to say our students reach for the stars. For example, a student uses six references instead of the required three, or a student uses the thesaurus and dictionary extensively to find vivid words to improve her sentences. The vivid words are evident in the product. At the other end of the scale, a one indicates that an element was not there at all. For example, the student didn't do any research, or the paragraphs contained a multitude of ideas, not just one.

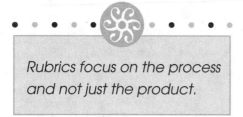

Rubrics focus on the process and not just the product.

We want students to know what we'll assess when we read their papers or view their projects, so we involve them when we develop rubrics. We begin by brainstorming everything we think should be included in the assessment. Then, through discussion, we weed out or add elements until we're all satisfied that we have a good assessment tool that will provide a fair evaluation.

Rubrics aren't just for teacher evaluations. We ask the students to use them to self-evaluate before they present their final product. If they discover that they've left something out or if something is not evident, they can go back and make corrections. When it's time for teacher evaluation, we use a copy of the rubric to make our assessment. It's always interesting to compare the students' rubrics with ours. They tend to be much harder on themselves.

Here are samples of the Editing Checklist, as well as rubrics we've used to evaluate poetry and report writing.

Editing Checklist

	Author	Editor
Ideas and Content		
My ideas are clear.	Yes ___ No ___	Yes ___ No ___
I give enough details.	Yes ___ No ___	Yes ___ No ___
I need to add information in these places:		

_____

_____

	Author	Editor
Organization		
My paper has a main idea.	Yes ___ No ___	Yes ___ No ___
Paragraphs only talk about one thing.	Yes ___ No ___	Yes ___ No ___
My paper has a strong beginning.	Yes ___ No ___	Yes ___ No ___
My ending is well thought out.	Yes ___ No ___	Yes ___ No ___
My paper doesn't jump around.	Yes ___ No ___	Yes ___ No ___
Topic sentences tell about each paragraph.	Yes ___ No ___	Yes ___ No ___
Voice		
This paper sounds like me.	Yes ___ No ___	Yes ___ No ___
This paper shows I care about the topic.	Yes ___ No ___	Yes ___ No ___
This paper is lively or exciting in some way, or it is a little different from everyone else's.	Yes ___ No ___	Yes ___ No ___
Descriptive Words		
I chose accurate, strong, specific words.	Yes ___ No ___	Yes ___ No ___
My words are fun to read.	Yes ___ No ___	Yes ___ No ___
Sentence Structure		
My sentences are smooth and easy to read.	Yes ___ No ___	Yes ___ No ___
Sentences start in different ways.	Yes ___ No ___	Yes ___ No ___
I have some long sentences and some short sentences to make my paper interesting.	Yes ___ No ___	Yes ___ No ___
Mechanics		
I checked my spelling.	Yes ___ No ___	Yes ___ No ___
I checked my capitals, periods, and indents.	Yes ___ No ___	Yes ___ No ___
I put quotation marks around what the person said.	Yes ___ No ___	Yes ___ No ___

Author signature .... Date ....

Editor's signature .... Date ....

The Best Research Reports Ever *Scholastic Professional Books, 1998*

Evaluating My Poetry

Name .... Date ....

Score	Description
5	Beyond expectation—I went way beyond what was expected.
4	Met the expectations—I applied skills as was expected.
3	Almost there—I had minor problems or omissions.
2	Not quite there—I had major problems or omissions.
1	Not there—I did not complete this part of the assignment.

1 2 3 4 5   I used at least three references in my research. They were:

_____

_____

_____

_____.

1 2 3 4 5   I completed a note-taking grid.

1 2 3 4 5   I had two students help me with revisions and editing.

1 2 3 4 5   My poem contains at least four facts.

1 2 3 4 5   I have a title for my poem, and I wrote it correctly.

1 2 3 4 5   The finished product is typed or neatly written.

1 2 3 4 5   My words are spelled correctly.

1 2 3 4 5   I followed the guidelines for the type of poetry I wrote.

(quatrain, couplets, free verse, _____)
other

Comments: _____

_____

_____

The Best Research Reports Ever *Scholastic Professional Books, 1998*

The Best Research Reports Ever *Scholastic Professional Books, 1998*

Evaluating My Writing

Name .... Date ....

Title of my writing ....

Rating Scale
5 = I did my best work and more than was expected.
4 = I did my best work and what was expected.
3 = I did not always do my best work.
2 = I did not do my best work.
1 = I did not complete this part of the assignment.
NA= not applicable (It could not be done with the type of writing I chose.)

1 2 3 4 5 NA   I used at least three references in my research.

1 2 3 4 5 NA   I took notes on my topic before I wrote about it.

1 2 3 4 5 NA   I wrote a rough draft and revised and edited it with two partners.

1 2 3 4 5 NA   I wrote an interesting title, and I wrote it correctly.

1 2 3 4 5 NA   I wrote a catchy beginning.

1 2 3 4 5 NA   I used the thesaurus to search for at least three vivid words.

1 2 3 4 5 NA   I used capital letters correctly.

1 2 3 4 5 NA   I indented my paragraphs.

1 2 3 4 5 NA   I wrote topic sentences for my paragraphs.

1 2 3 4 5 NA   I spelled all words correctly.

1 2 3 4 5 NA   I have included a bibliography, and I wrote it correctly.

The Best Research Reports Ever *Scholastic Professional Books, 1998*

Progress Checklists

Staying on task or sticking to a time line is difficult for some students. We work with each student individually to establish time lines, since some students need more time for in-depth research than others or have chosen more difficult projects. However, some students need written step by step directions in any case. Pam Newton, a teacher at Wingate Elementary, developed the progress checklist on the next page.

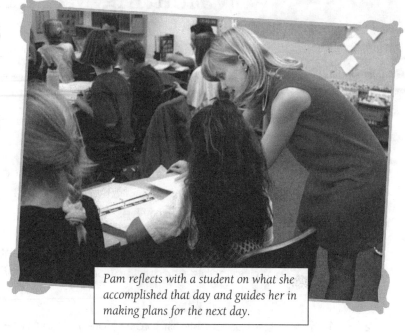

Pam reflects with a student on what she accomplished that day and guides her in making plans for the next day.

As mentioned in Chapter Four (page 60), our students complete a daily self-evaluation form when they are working on a project. They reflect on what they accomplished, self-evaluate their work for the day, and make plans for next time. There is also a column where they can ask for help. A quick look through these forms helps us determine mini-lessons that we need to teach or assistance we need to give to an individual. It also helps a student stay focused.

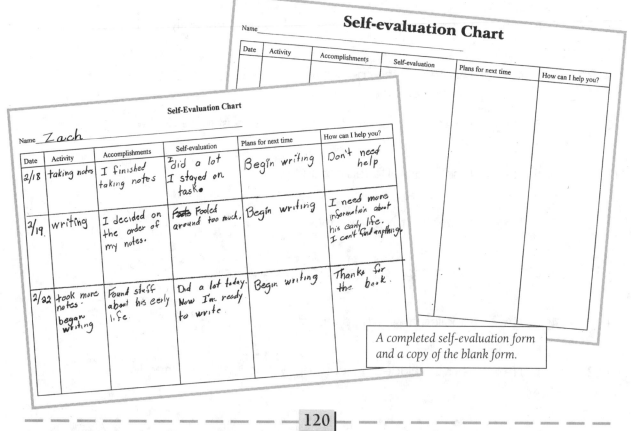

A completed self-evaluation form and a copy of the blank form.

The Best Research Reports Ever *Scholastic Professional Books, 1998*

Progress Check for Your
Writing Assignment

Name .... Date ....

This paper is due ....

You'll need to:

_____ Use at least two reference books.

_____ Use a note-taking grid when you take notes.

_____ Write your draft skipping every other line.

_____ Revise your draft, checking to see if you have an interesting introduction.

_____ Do you have at least six historical facts in your journal?

_____ Revise with a friend. Use the editing checklist to guide you. Get your partner's signature on your paper.

_____ Reread your paper and revise and edit as necessary.

_____ Publish your paper.

_____ Read your paper again. Check for errors.

_____ Evaluate your paper, using the rubric.

The Best Research Reports Ever *Scholastic Professional Books, 1998*

Teacher Conferences

Often we have a student bring her research notes to a conference so we can discuss them together. We ask the student to explain the process she used to write the notes. Sometimes we have the student use her notes to discuss the topic of research. Other times we'll work on the introductory or concluding paragraphs together. Students need to see that we are interested in their research, note-taking, drafting, and revising, as well as the final product. Writing brief notes on an anecdotal record sheet during a conference helps us remember details about each student's progress.

> *Students need to see that we are interested in their research, note-taking, and drafting as well as the final product*

Student Evaluations

Besides the daily self-evaluation sheets students fill out, they write self-evaluations when they've finished their research projects. They explain what they've learned and what the projects demonstrate they can do. They can also set goals for self-improvement. Reflecting on what they've accomplished and learned makes the learning process more meaningful.

Jimmer's evaluation of his poem about a coyote. Only part of his poem is visible, as the evaluation is on top of it.

Emily's writing evaluation about her poem.

122

Portfolios

A student portfolio is a yearlong process. As students work, they save notes, outlines, drafts, final copies, and pictures of their final projects. At least four times a year we have our students go through the material they've saved and select a sample or samples of their best work to include in their portfolio. We encourage our students to include notes and drafts with a final paper so that all the steps are included. The student portfolio shows progress and development over time, and students take pride in their work as they review their portfolios. (See *Portfolios in the Classroom*, by Joan Clemmons and Lois Laase, et al., Scholastic, 1993, for more detailed information about portfolios.)

Amy and Lauren organize their portfolios.

Parent Comments and Evaluation

We've found that it's important to involve parents in the evaluation process and that they like to be involved. Still, many of them don't have a schedule that allows them time to visit or volunteer, so we find ways to involve them anyway. For example, after students have completed a class book like the one discussed in Chapter Three, we put it in an envelope with a routing slip on the outside. Each night a different student takes the book home and shares it with his parents. We encourage our parents to write comments on the routing slip. Some of the comments we have received include: "This is truly outstanding! It is a great way to learn while having fun." "It's a great way to learn...for all of us! Thanks for letting me be a part of your class." This is a wonderful way to keep parents aware of their children's progress.

> *The portfolio shows progress and development over time.*

We frequently videotape our students' oral presentations so they can take them home. The parents and student view the video and together complete an assessment rubric we've sent with it. (See a sample oral presentation rubric on the following page.)

> *Parents like to be involved with the activities at school, yet many of them do not have a schedule that allows them time to visit or volunteer.*

The Best Research Reports Ever   *Scholastic Professional Books, 1998*

Oral Presentation Assessment

Name .... Date ....

Title of Speech ....

Watch your video with your parents or another adult. Check your speaking skills using the following checklist. Be sure you do not rewind your tape. It should be ready to tape the next time.

When speaking I...

speak loud and clear.	Yes ☐	Sometimes ☐	No ☐
speak with expression.	Yes ☐	Sometimes ☐	No ☐
make eye contact with my audience.	Yes ☐	Sometimes ☐	No ☐
hold my paper still and below my face.	Yes ☐	Sometimes ☐	No ☐
sit or stand straight.	Yes ☐	Sometimes ☐	No ☐
concentrate on what I am saying.	Yes ☐	Sometimes ☐	No ☐

I am proud of the way I _____

_____.

Next time I will try to improve _____

_____.

Signature of parent(s) or person(s) evaluating this tape with me.

_____

Comments _____

_____

_____

The Best Research Reports Ever *Scholastic Professional Books, 1998*

We do welcome parents to visit and volunteer. For those parents who can volunteer regularly, we establish regular schedules for them to assist children with their work and assessments. Some parents are more comfortable with doing clerical help, such as running off papers or cutting construction paper. Others enjoy working directly with the students. It's always nice to have a parent around when the students are working on big projects. Frequently these projects spill out into

Parent volunteer helps a student check the spelling of a word in a dictionary

the hallway where supervision is necessary. We also have parents who assist the students with the different stages of writing, such as using the thesaurus, locating references, or even reading difficult material. If parents volunteer in a classroom it is important that we make them feel welcome and show that we appreciate their help.

> *The knowledge we gain from using these assessment tools drives our instructional program.*

Using these assessment tools helps us understand the development and progress of each of our students. The knowledge we gain from using them drives our instructional program. We wish we had a magic formula for translating the information we glean from the tools into grades for a report card, but we do not. Nevertheless, we have discovered that using the tools provides us with a good basis for determining final grades and the data to support our decisions.

The Best Research Reports Ever *Scholastic Professional Books, 1998*

Research Is a Journey

Through this book, we hope that we have shown that research is a journey for which students need guidance. By teaching research skills, we are giving them the tools they need to develop into independent learners. These skills not only prepare students for the academic challenges that await them, they prepare students for life.

Our goal for this book is to help you guide students to see that research is more than just amassing facts on a subject; it is a multilevel process involving any number of resources and myriad thinking skills. Research requires a student to sort, reflect, and synthesize information in a manner that transforms the raw data into something uniquely the student's own. Only then does acquiring knowledge result in a deeper understanding of a subject and a broader view of the world.

We hope you can incorporate our ideas into your curriculum. We wish you well on your own classroom journey.

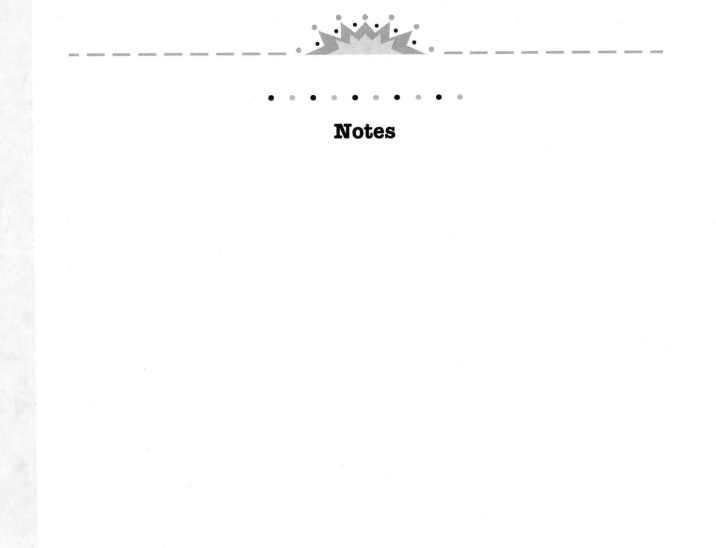

Notes

The Best Research Reports Ever   *Scholastic Professional Books, 1998*

Notes

The Best Research Reports Ever   *Scholastic Professional Books, 1998*